Last Days of
Steam on the LMS & BR

Last Days of
Steam on the LMS & BR

A Railwayman's Memoirs

Roderick H. Fowkes

HALSGROVE

First published in Great Britain in 2009

Copyright © R.H. Fowkes 2009

Individual photographs remain the copyright of the respective copyright holders.

British Library Cataloguing-in-Publication Data
A CIP record for this title is available from the British Library

ISBN 978 1 84114 976 9

HALSGROVE
Halsgrove House,
Ryelands Industrial Estate,
Bagley Road, Wellington, Somerset TA21 9PZ
Tel: 01823 653777   Fax: 01823 216796
email: sales@halsgrove.com

Part of the Halsgrove group of companies
Information on all Halsgrove titles is available at: www.halsgrove.com

Printed and bound by CPI Antony Rowe, Wiltshire

Contents

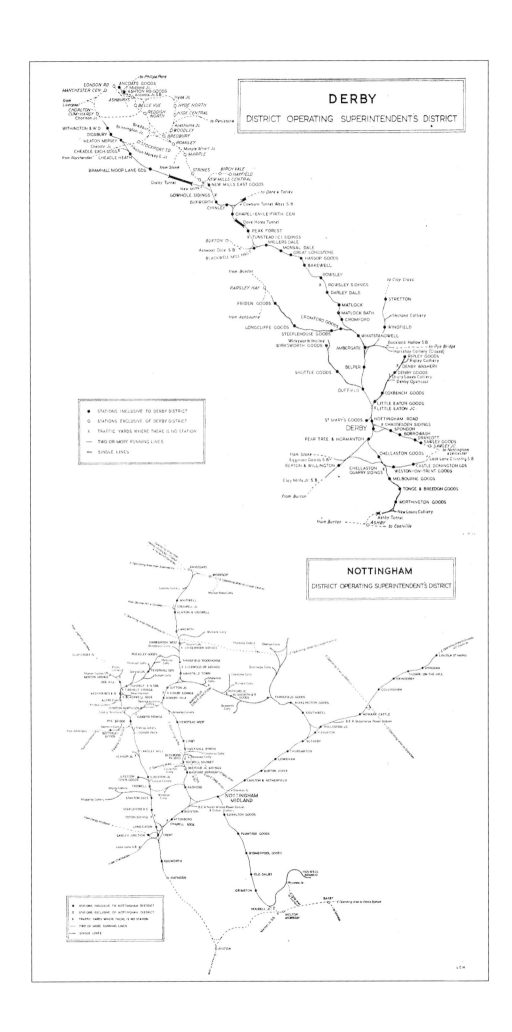

Introduction

Before retiring from British Rail in March 1996 as Movements and Planning Manager at Laira Traction and Maintenance Depot in Plymouth, I well remember a conversation with Paul Furtek of Locomaster Profiles fame shortly after being appointed to that position in January 1991. Paul had come to the depot for a meeting with Geoff Hudson the Area Fleet Manager regarding the making of a video of the English Electric Class 50 diesel locomotives that were having their swan song on the Exeter-Waterloo services. After acquainting Paul, that, before moving to Plymouth I had been Traction Arranger at Toton Traction Maintenance Depot, Europe's largest installation where the "Peak" diesels were prevalent. "Why don't you chronicle your reminiscences – from the inside looking out?" he retorted.

I was born in 1941 at Breaston, a village midway between Derby and Nottingham, a couple of miles from Toton, the largest marshalling yard in Britain. The youngest of three children and the only one with an interest in the railway that began at an early age, no doubt prompted and encouraged by my mother, the daughter of a stationmaster, who accompanied me for the first time to Tamworth and Crewe. Long before that it would be over the fields spending hours alongside the Midland Main Line, watching the trains go by. As a young boy I often reflected standing on the platform at Derby station observing the driver operating the handle of the water column after his fireman had put the 'bag' in the tender of an express for London or the West Country. Whilst this was in progress the driver would then proceed to give more than a cursory glance over the engine. Filled up, often to overflowing, the next opportunity to take water would be the water troughs on the approaches to Tamworth (going west) or Loughborough (southwards). Now with both back on the footplate, and any trainspotters who might have been fortunate in being allowed onto the engine during the brief stop being ushered back onto the platform. After tending too his fire the fireman would then eagerly look for the right-away from the platform, a whistle from the locomotive up would go the regulator and often with a deafening roar the express moved away. These interludes involving proud individuals with cherry blossom boots, often with a collar and tie left me with a mounting desire to be an engine driver. But, it didn't quite turn out like that.

A school outing in 1954 was my first visit to London, the impression of St. Pancras being firmly etched in my memory, a spectacular memorial to the days of the Midland Railway. We have to thank the poet laureate John Betjeman who was successful in his campaign to save the station from closure in the 1960s.

Those halcyon school days when delivering newspapers in freezing conditions and having hot aches in the fingers, the bicycle going anywhere but where it was supposed to in the deep ruts of ice and snow, also those pea-souper freezing fogs, which didn't dissipate for days on end. All change of course during the summer months, when it was daylight until eleven o'clock at night with double summer time.

Left to my own devices, I can't ever remember having a conversation with my father regarding my schoolwork and he showed absolutely no interest at all regarding my future employment. As reflected in the book he railroaded my elder brother into wasted years on the Co-op milk round when Ivor himself would have preferred an apprenticeship. My sister Diana (Jane), I suspect, also had to make her own way in the world, such was the lack of interest shown and it was left to mother to mend any fences.

I am deeply indebted to George Mellors, a friendly porter at Draycott & Breaston station who was instrumental in my joining the railway. In December 1956 whilst showing me how to knock back into shape the crank on my bicycle he told me about the vacancy at Trent for a junior porter, a position I had turned down some five months earlier. Despite ending up on the Great Western for the last eighteen years of a 39-year career, I will always be associated with being a Midland Man through and through.

In this book, and any potential follow up, I have attempted to describe the fun it can be working with a cross section of characters, whilst the intransigence of others often led to displeasure. Avoiding a detailed history of locomotives and the L.M.S. Railway, which has been covered elsewhere in greater detail. The illustrations chosen have been kindly supplied by Alan (Joe) Wade and Warren (A.W.) Smith, to both I extend my gratitude, in particular to Mr Wade a gentleman who moved to Long Eaton from Yorkshire, who, with his 'walking permit' for railway premises took photographs around the Liverpool area prior to Nationalisation in 1948. My first meeting with Joe was as a result of four photographs of closed stations in the area that appeared in the weekly *Long Eaton Advertiser*. As he was ex-directory I rang the editor of the newspaper and she made contact with Joe, as I was keen to access his photographs.

R.H. Fowkes
Devon 2009

Sawley Station which closed in 1930, where the author's grandfather was stationmaster.

One
The Early Years

"That's a sign of rain", a cliché echoed by my mother on many occasions when the sounds of wheels on rail joints appearing to emanate from just across the road instead of the half-mile or so on the London Midland Region, Derby to London railway line. With the prevailing westerly wind enhancing the sounds of trains, it was not surprising that their passing could clearly be heard, although on occasions the prophecy must have had some credence.

* * *

The cosy little cottage on The Green in Breaston – where according to some, was where illicit dealings took place – two up, two down, with no electricity, an adjoining wash-house and toilet, linked to a large two roomed coal-house with two upper storeys in turn joined onto our gas lit living accommodation. An oak beamed living room with open fire complete with range, oven and boiler all requiring black-leading at intervals. No sink or running water, hence the washhouse down the yard, rainwater from an outside water butt was fed into the boiler and this provided the necessary hot water for washing. Rain-water, according to my mother was better than tap water for washing the hair and a sprig of rosemary in the final rinse would produce a fine sheen. Sunday of course was bath night, ready for school the following day; this was in the form of a large tin bath in front of the fire, with two buckets of rainwater heated on the gas stove. There was no heating at all upstairs; indeed, only one of the bedrooms had a gas light with an adjustable flame. During extremely cold weather an oven shelf wrapped in a blanket supplemented the hot water bottle. We had a selection of animals, a couple of ducks, some hens whose eggs were religiously dated by mum, and no less than five cats all female. Two of them would take it in turns to sit on the boiler often singeing their tails whilst turning around, usually though they had the best seats in the house. On Saturdays it was a regular feature for them to sit around the lamppost in the middle of The Green, waiting for mother to return from the Co-op butchers some fifty yards away. The cats appeared to be aware that a supply of 'lights' was imminent, usually eaten raw, although a couple of them getting on in years had it boiled, and my goodness didn't it smell. On the pavement outside our garden stood a telegraph pole, one day a dog chased one of the cats, Jim, who was almost eighteen years old and she clambered almost to the top of the pole. When about eight feet from the top on her way down, the cat lost her footing and fell to the pavement. Jim's tongue was cut almost through and it was protruding from her mouth, the cat went missing for a number of days and was seemingly none the worse for her ordeal when she reappeared. A weekly rent of seven shillings, (35p in today's values), was paid to a local farmer. I well remember those heady haymaking days when Bonnie and Flower provided the necessary horsepower with the loaded hay carts, and with double summer time in evidence, in those days it did not get dark until after eleven o'clock.

Not having electricity meant that we could not have television; it was not until the Coronation in 1953 that TV sets became more readily available. Nonetheless there was a 'friend in the corner', which was a source of entertainment, namely a wireless. It was a huge contraption, with a large Vidor battery, big valves and an accumulator. Care had to be exercised to ensure the spare accumulator was kept fully charged, otherwise we could find that we could not get any sound. At an early age I listened fanatically to the wireless, sifting through the Radio Times; the latter, I recall, was recycled, finding its way into the small room at the end of the week. The mellifluous voices of the announcers and news-readers gripped my imagination – the revered tones of Stuart Hibberd, John Snagge, Frank Phillips and Alvar Liddell, the legendary radiomen of that era. Immediately following Dick Barton on the then Light Programme came Radio Newsreel at seven o'clock with Imperial Echoes as its signature tune. That half hour of news with reports from around the world by renowned correspondents, the likes of Erik de Mauny in Moscow, Gerald Priestland in Washington, Charles Wheeler in New York and Antony Lawrence in South East Asia became household names, as had the announcers and news-readers during the war years. Radio Luxembourg was an alternative to the BBC and provided such programmes as Double Your Money and Take Your Pick both of which transferred very successfully to Independent Television. Features also included Perry Mason and The Scarlet Pimpernel; the one overriding problem in listening to the station of course was the fading signal.

Entering the house during darkness could be slightly hazardous, walking through the only door into a reception area bounded by a cellar, one had to negotiate their way into the living room towards the shelf above the fireplace, avoiding the gas light suspended from an oak beam, where the matches were usually kept. Many times one's head came into contact with the globe and the mantle would break, it was always the policy to keep a few spare mantles to cover this eventuality. Often, people reflect that the good old days were not that good, indeed, they may be right, but reflecting back to those gas lit days it wasn't all that bad. Families made their own entertainment, although dad was out at the pub every night the adage that television killed the art of conversation cannot be denied. My father was a warehouse foreman at the Long Eaton Co-op; and he also acted as bookie's runner for Harold Dykes who ran the Regal Club in Long Eaton. Those illicit dealings, whereby the level of interest generated by horse racing was considerable and on big race days the Grand National and the Derby produced huge amounts of stake money. Even the local policeman – Bobby Mackay – was not averse to having a flutter. What annoyed my mother intensely were the punters who came round on a Sunday morning to collect their winnings when the betting slips had not been returned from the bookie. Dad incidentally, had railroaded my elder brother who was looking for an apprenticeship in the years prior to his call up for national service, into a wasted period on the Co-op milk round. There was to be no such fate with my employment, or was there?

* * *

Jabez (Jim) Wright was the landlord of the Chequers Inn on The Green, and being friendly with the landlord's son Dennis, we would sort empty bottles in the cellar from the night before that were all returnable.

How I wish I had kept some of the discarded cigarette packets of that era, Craven A, Kensitas, Park Drive, Players Weights, Senior Service, State Express, Turf and Wood-bine to name but a few. It was at the Chequers Inn that I first saw a television, albeit a 9" screen, where children's series on the television would include The Lone Ranger, Cisco Kid, Hopalong Cassidy, Kit Carson and Gene Autry; these could also be seen at the cinemas in nearby Long Eaton on a Saturday afternoon. People went to the pictures a lot in those days, my mother always liked a good cowboy film and some of the ' B' westerns of the forties and early fifties were always well received. On a Saturday evening we would queue outside the Scala or Palace cinemas to enjoy what in some cases would be just the supporting film. There was a third cinema in Long Eaton, the Empire, known as the fleapit; I don't recollect my mother ever taking me there.

* * *

From the austere days of the early Nationalisation era, images of both locomotives and rolling stock were continually changing. During the transitional period a few locomotives from the Big Four were turned out in various shades of green and blue, no doubt to gauge the public reaction alongside the coaching stock. Also in evidence was the lettering BRITISH RAILWAYS in full on the tender, which would remain until the adoption of the 'Lion and Wheel' totem in 1949. Often referred to as the 'ferret and dartboard' this was replaced in 1956 by 'a demi-lion rampant with a silver locomotive wheel held between the paws emerging from a heraldic crown complete with insignias of Great Britain', with a British Railways legend. The emblem was also displayed on coaching stock. Never having witnessed an 8P (Coronation/Gresley A4) engine in blue livery, those handsome and extremely powerful locomotives were soon to be adorned in BR Brunswick Green, already applied to other locos in the higher power ranges. The LMR however in 1957 adopted a maroon colour for their ex-LMS Pacifics thereby transforming those great engines. Coaching stock values also changed with some embellished in experimental liveries. The 'Plum and Spilt Milk' colour of the main-line corridor coaches gave way to 'Crimson Lake and Cream', also referred to as 'Blood and Custard'. Restored to a limited extent in 1954 by the then British Transport Commission, who decreed that Corporate Liveries – Chocolate and Cream for the Western, Green for the Southern – within limitations be reintroduced, which in 1957 became the norm. Gradually (SR excepted) Maroon livery was to be the uniform colour throughout until the mid 1960s when Blue with Grey upper panels would become standard.

* * *

In 1950 my brother joined the forces, his eighteen-month stint in the Royal Army Medical Corps being extended to two years owing to the Korean War, he was hospitalised for a while and had a spell at Netley recuperating. When home on forty-eight hour leave, Ivor would return to his base at Aldershot, travelling back on the 6 p.m. train from Derby to St. Pancras on a Sunday evening. At my mothers insistence we would walk down the dark and unlit lane to Sawley Crossing in the vain hope of getting a glimpse of him as the train flashed by in the darkness, all to no avail though as a solitary gas lamp each side of the crossing provided the only illumination.

What a surprise it was a few years earlier for a six and a half year old lad whose mother had taken him down the lane to Sawley Crossing to watch the trains go by, when a strange phenomena occurred. Peering through that same wicker gate protecting the railway line,

Johnson Midland Class 2F 0-6-0 No 58125 on a local trip working to Chaddesden passing Sawley level crossing, *circa* 1950.

fully expecting the roar of a steam engine to come thundering past, when, out of the blue without warning, this elegant black and silver monster growled by, those LMS letters shining with brilliant lustre, catching the eye more so than the number 10000. It was the first main line diesel-electric locomotive to be built in Britain, LMS-designed, Co-Co No.10000 emerged from Derby Locomotive Works on 5th December 1947 followed by its twin No.10001 the following July. Resplendent in black livery with silver waistband and numbers (also LMS in the case of 10000) they looked a picture at the head of an express. The 1,600hp locomotives, often working in pairs, did their initial proving runs on the Midland Main Line to St. Pancras before being allocated to Camden where they would have charge of the 'Royal Scot' out of Euston.

Another emergence from the same Workshops in July 1950, with a chequered career was the infamous diesel-mechanical 4-8-4 Fell locomotive No. 10100. After exhaustive testing locally and further modifications it worked a variety of trains on the Midland Main Line but saw most of its short working life, when not in the Works, operating between Derby and Manchester Central. It was at that location in 1958, only seven years after its introduction, that the locomotive train-heating boiler caught fire, seriously damaging the diesel resulting in its withdrawal. The Southern built 1Co-Co1 diesel-electric locomotives Nos.10201 + 10202 (1,750hp) and 10203 (2,000hp) also worked between Derby and the metropolis in the 1950s and all three had spells in the Works at Derby. By 1956 the three ex- Southern locomotives had also been transferred to the Western Division again working out of Euston.

*   *   *

Brought up on a diet of 'Jubilee' and Stanier Class '5' 4-6-0 locomotives from the depots at Millhouses (Sheffield), Holbeck (Leeds), Trafford Park (Manchester), Kentish Town (London), Derby and Nottingham, they were the standard first line motive power on the expresses to and from St. Pancras, still assisted on occasions by Compound 4-4-0s. Local trains being in the hands of ex-Midland Class '2' 4-4-0s or Fowler and Stanier 2-6-4 tanks. Freight traffic was handled by Stanier 2-8-0s and the mighty Beyer-Garratts, the odd Austerity plus a multitude of Midland type 0-6-0s, many of which lasted almost until the end of steam in the area. A variation to this was the daily working of unrebuilt 'Patriot' No. 45509 'The Derbyshire Yeomanry' which for a brief spell was allocated to Derby (17A), and regularly worked the 7.35 a.m. Nottingham-Bristol. The usual Holbeck engine appeared on the afternoon Cricklewood-Derby St. Mary's – en-route Carlisle – milk empties, whilst a Midland Class 4F 0-6-0 invariably worked the evening lettuce train. One freight that often provided a locomotive from north of the border was the 4.25 p.m. Class 'C' Leicester-Carlisle fully-fitted, often referred to as the 'Boxer', a 'Jubilee' or Stanier Class '5' with the customary (St. Rollox) enlarged numerals was always well received. Another working that occasionally produced a Glasgow based 'Jubilee' was a Sunday afternoon filling-in turn with a local Derby-Nottingham passenger train which returning later in the evening.

In the early 1950s, to the delight of train spotters there was an Anglo-Scottish transfer of half-a-dozen long serving 'Jubilees' between the Midland Division and depots at Kingmoor (Carlisle), Perth and Glasgow. Other unusual visitors were locomotives for overhaul at Derby Locomotive Works; which would include those from East London (Plaistow 33A) often finding their way down, dead in a freight train from Wellingborough. Locomotives when out-shopped would often have a trial run from Derby to Trent via the North Curve and back.

*   *   *

Who would argue with the adage that school days are the best times of your life? No sooner had we trooped in for morning assembly when, just over a quarter of a mile away, a 'Jubilee' would rattle by at ten minutes past nine with an express for London. Scant regard was paid to the music teacher when the lunchtime freight from Toton to Chaddesden went by hauled by a Beyer-Garratt. All down road trains (towards Derby), except

Freshly outshopped from Derby Locomotive Works on a proving run in August 1952, 'Johnson' 0-4-4T No. 58089 of Plaistow M.P.D (33A) waits at Trent on the 2nd Up passenger line for a path back to Derby.
J.A. Wade

The driver of Beyer-Garratt 2-6-6-2T No. 47996 gives a friendly wave as his train, a lunchtime Toton-Chaddesden freight, approaches Sawley Crossing in July 1955.
J.A. Wade

(Below, left) Paired with a Fowler high sided narrow 3,500 gallon, 5½ ton capacity tender, 'Jubilee' No. 45646 '*Napier*' nearing Sawley Crossing in July 1955 with a Manchester-St. Pancras express.
J.A. Wade

(Right) This November 1957 picture shows the site of the station at Sawley opened in 1839. My grandfather was stationmaster there until its closure in 1930. It was originally called 'Breaston'.
J.A. Wade

those via Way & Works, whistled a routing at Sawley Crossing and these could clearly be heard. The practice of the driver using his whistle to send a message to the signalman, using so many 'pops or crows' as a direction code, was commonplace all over the railway system. The Chaddesden trundled past with an endless stream of wagons; to be followed in the opposite direction by another 'Jubilee' hauled express for St. Pancras.

At a very early age, like so many other boys of my generation, I wanted to be an engine driver. My father was less than enthusiastic about the idea, but my mother – who came from a good railway family Harvey – was all for it. Her father had been stationmaster at

The '*Harvey*' Clan

Sawley until the station closed in 1930 and two of her brothers were also railway employees. It was no doubt her interest in railway matters that she first escorted me to Crewe, spending hours in the refreshment and waiting rooms whilst I dashed hither and thither around the station in an effort not to miss a single movement. In addition to Crewe my mother also accompanied me to Tamworth, for sheer volume of trains that place took some beating, it was a paradise for trainspotters. Owing to their great number, enthusiasts were banished from the station platforms in the late 1940s, from where they sought sanctuary in a nearby field adjacent to the downside low-level platform. From that vantage point it was difficult to obtain the numbers of locomotives on high-level trains, as they were obscured by the station buildings, normally one or two individuals would race to the far end of the field where a clear view could be obtained and then return to disseminate the information to the waiting crowd. The high-level boasted a named train, albeit one, 'The Devonian', usual motive power being a Leeds (Holbeck) or Bristol (Barrow Road) 'Jubilee', the occasional un-rebuilt 'Patriot' or in the case of a Stanier Class '5' where an assist locomotive would often be provided. Beyer-Garratts were also in evidence on long freight trains plying their way between Toton and Washwood Heath and they always produced a degree of excitement amongst the spotters. Most however, myself included, came to Tamworth to see the largest classes of ex-LMS steam-power. Legendary named trains complete with headboards, 'The Comet', 'The Irish Mail', 'The Lakes Express', 'The Mancunian', 'The Manxman', 'The Merseyside Express', 'The Mid-Day Scot', 'The Red Rose', 'The Shamrock', 'The Welshman', 'The Ulster Express', and, grandest of all, 'The Royal Scot'.

Some expresses often loaded up to sixteen carriages and their thundering through the low-level fast lines was truly a sight to behold, the two routes where the London & North Western passed below the Midland having an abundance of traffic. An early indication of an impending train on the low-level was heralded by cries of 'Clanger', 'Main', 'Baby Clanger' or 'Baby Main', everyone's attention would then be focused on the matter in hand. Expectations often turning to disappointment with utterances of scrap it as a commoner charged through. Situated immediately outside the station was a cafe, where even the hardiest soul sought refuge during inclement weather, I suspect that the proprietor became a rich man judging by the numbers of train spotters visiting Tamworth.

'Britannia' Pacfic 4-6-2 No. 70033 *Charles Dickens* awaits departure from Tamworth Low Level with a Manchester London Road-Euston express, circa 1955.

My mother, bless her heart often reflected to me later, how on the occasion she took me there, that in order to while away the time before the train home, she would often walk down the same streets in Tamworth more than once. Those were things, which you do not appreciate at the time. The 9.9 a.m. from Derby (8.6 a.m. Sheffield-Gloucester) was the train favoured by many train spotters going to Tamworth for the day, returning late afternoon by the 2.15 p.m. Bristol-York. Even that resulted in a relatively early start from my local station arriving back shortly after six o'clock in the evening.

One Sunday morning, a few years later, together with a couple of pals we set off on our bicycles on the 48 mile round trip to Tamworth via the notorious steep hill at Measham. Settling ourselves down at a spot adjacent to a railway overbridge at around lunchtime overlooking a set of water troughs, we eagerly awaited the approach of a Stanier Pacific, thundering by with its tender overflowing. After a while, the steady beat of a Stanier engine could be heard coming from the direction of the overbridge. Our position on the top of the embankment precluded us from seeing the locomotive until it passed underneath the bridge. It turned out to be a 'Jubilee' from Bristol Barrow Road shed and our expectations were further dashed when the identifying boards on the coaches portrayed Bristol – York.

Unwittingly, we had lost our bearings and stationed ourselves on the Midland line at the water troughs on the approach to Tamworth and not as we thought on the trackside of the L.N.W.R. A detour then took us to the low-level lines at Tamworth, being a Sunday of course the trains were non-too frequent and after finding solace in the cafe outside the station we embarked on the long journey back home.

An essential piece of equipment in those days of course was the Ian Allan abc, supplemented with the monthly 'Trains Illustrated'. I well remember also buying the combined edition of the abc at ten shillings (50p) although the Southern and Western regions did not interest me at that time. An evening newspaper round realised seven shillings and sixpence a week (38p in today's value), and later a morning round which paid twice the amount, was then worked in tandem with the delivery of groceries for Marsden, an outlet long since disappeared. Those activities provided the necessary funds for the Ian Allan abc and Trains Illustrated as well as future trips to Tamworth and Crewe. An American schoolteacher from Montana, over on a temporary secondment showed an interested

In need of a trouser press, the author aged 14 years at Tamworth with an American teacher.

in steam engines, so what better place to take him, but to Tamworth. He also had an appointment one day in Manchester and I took time off school to accompany him.

A day trip to Blackpool was not without incident. I lost a valuable piece of reference, my notebook with a considerable amount of numbers that had not been entered into my Ian Allan abc. I remembered balancing the notebook beneath the window in the carriage door, when releasing the window by the strap the book dropped down the aperture within the door casing. Thinking back, if the window had then been hoisted back up, maybe the notebook would have reappeared.

After school during daylight hours and at weekends, long before being allowed out to either Tamworth or Crewe on my own, it was the Midland Main Line serving Derby and St. Pancras to Nottingham that provided the insight for train spotting. A footpath led from the village of Breaston to Church Wilne, across the fields, and it was by way of this, that along with others would ensconce us amid the thirteen willow trees alongside the Golden Brook. The trees being climbed on numerous occasions, or a spot of net fishing in the brook being just two of the pastimes whilst awaiting the passage of trains, not to mention the odd piece of ballast targeted at the white insular pots on the telegraph poles. Whether there, or at Sawley Crossing there was no shortage of pyrotechnics on the 1-in-474/815 rising gradient as trains recovered from the slowings of the Trent curves, those which were double-headed being quite spectacular. An indication of an impending train was by the observance of the signals controlled from the signal box at Draycott. However, on a Sunday when that 'box was switched out, reliance was focused on the distant signal operated from the signal box at Sawley Crossing, which together with the down starting signal was operated from the same 'box. The fields on either side of the footpath were where farmer 'Waggy' West had a dozen cows; it was often a case of dodging their pats when dashing from the trees to the line side. One Sunday evening some of his beasts managed to stray onto the railway line and were killed by the six o'clock express from Derby. Word had it that Mr West was observed sitting on the rail in tears.

The Golden Brook, a placid stream would, after periods of heavy and prolonged rain turn into a raging torrent, collecting water off the nearby Risley hills flooding neighbouring farmland with West Park at Long Eaton also coming under water. It wasn't unusual for the B6005 Derby-Nottingham road to be flooded at Breaston outside the surgery of Doctor Christie. The railway line did not escape either, on the west side of

Draycott & Breaston station the line would become impassable with trains being diverted to and from Derby via Melbourne Junction and Chellaston over the Castle Donington branch to Sheet Stores Junction, a feature still happening to this day, diverted trains now however have to reverse at Stenson Junction to gain accession to the branch line. In 1996 Railtrack had a complete blockade of the line at Draycott in order to take remedial action to alleviate the flooding of the line, a new pipe being installed to carry water into the nearby River Derwent.

One afternoon whilst train spotting at Sawley Crossing it started to rain quite sharply, as there was nowhere to shelter the friendly signalman realising my plight, invited me into the 'box, his name, Derek Blount.

He turned out to be a relief signalman and I visited him at other signal boxes where he worked: Spondon Station, Spondon Junction and Turntable Sidings as well as Castle Donington. After a time I became pretty proficient in understanding the working of those installations. A few years later, Derek I believe emigrated to Australasia. Indeed, another signalman, Frank Derrick, a family friend, told me that owing to remedial work being undertaken in Milford tunnel between Derby and Ambergate, all trains during the night turn were being diverted from Derby via Trent and the Erewash valley. With this in mind, I spent a Friday night with Frank in the signal box at Draycott, only to find that the diversions were only applicable on Monday to Thursday nights.

Unauthorised incursion into Toton M.P.D. (18A) on Sunday afternoons was commonplace, the huge depot with its three roundhouses, Nos. 2 and 3 housing the through road for the mighty Beyer-Garratts, had an eerie perception about them. Inside the sheds steam engines stood forlorn looking, some with their smoke box doors open, others receiving attention but not on this day, the requisite 'Not to be moved' board in position. Those majestic machines stood silent, a few awaiting the arrival of the steam raiser with his supply of firelighters, in readiness for work on Monday morning. Access to the depot was over the Grand Union Canal continuing over the River Erewash before slipping around the back over a stream. On one occasion I was apprehended by a patrolling BTC policeman who noted my name and address and warned me about trespassing, after that episode, visits for a time became less frequent. A good vantage point could be had at the southern end of Toton sidings where a bridge (Long Tom) spanned the main and goods lines. Passenger services served local stations along the Erewash Valley between Nottingham and Sheffield, in addition to the 'Thames-Clyde Express',

Midland 0-6-0 Class 2F No. 58173 in one of the roundhouses at Toton M.P.D. in September 1957.
J.A. Wade

Class 3P 4-4-2T No. 41947 at Toton M.P.D. in July 1958. Of L.T. & S.R. design built by the L.M.S. after grouping.
J.A. Wade

Class 3P 4-4-2T No. 41947 at Toton M.P.D. in August 1958. A Midland and L.M.S. development of L.T. & S "79" Class.
J.A. Wade

there were also a couple of Bradford-London expresses, before they were re-routed from Trowell Junction via Nottingham and Melton Mowbray to St. Pancras. From the bridge one was literally only yards away from the high-level arrival lines with trains from Nottingham and the south, whilst on the low level, those from Chaddesden and the west would pass before being drawn back onto one of the high-level arrival lines by one or two 0-6-0 diesel shunting engines. Before hump shunting commenced the chalker would mark the wagon with the sorting sidings number, the couplings then being released by his colleague, and they would also service the brakevan. Steam engines that were not in the best of shape for whatever condition or waiting to go into the shops were employed locally. The duties usually involved the movement of crossroad traffic from the up side East yard to the down side and from the Meadow yard across to the up side. The loco also carried a target number on the buffer beam.

The annual horticultural show incorporating the Derby Locomotive Works Open Day always produced massive crowds. The star attraction being a locomotive not normally seen in the Derby area, that ranged from a 'Royal Scot' or a 'Britannia' in the early 1950s to the ultimate, a member of the 'Coronation' class, the likes of No. 46251 the appropriately named 'City of Nottingham' or 46256 'Sir William A. Stanier F.R.S'.

The neighbouring motive power depot was out of bounds to the visitors, cordoned off and patrolled by BTC police, despite this though, there were quite a number of spotters who found an alternative way in. Steam engines awaiting a berth in the Locomotive Works conglomerated in sidings adjacent to Deadmans Lane. In April 1951 the new BR

Standard Class '5' 4-6-0 No. 73000 appeared from the shops, those and other engines released ex-works often had a trial run to Trent and back. When arriving at Derby station by train from the south, it was nigh impossible to see the numbers of locos on shed that stood behind those in the front line. During the morning a raft of ex-works locomotives would be hauled out of one of the outside shed roads towards Engine Shed Sidings signal box before being propelled back again, their motions making a hissing noise although devoid of steam, nevertheless those were engines whose numbers had up to that point been unobtainable. Many train spotters positioned themselves at the southern end of platform 1. My preference being the south end of platform 6, from where a first hand view could be had of the engines on the NE/SW and London bound expresses taking water. Watching the fireman rebuilding his fire whilst the replenishing of the tender was being undertaken, often viewed from on the footplate, after the driver had responded to the request of, "Can I cab you driver please?" Enginemen were proud individuals, collar and tie and clean overalls, cherry blossom boots. There was nothing else that I would want to do on leaving school, than to be an engine driver.

Visits to Crewe Locomotive Works were permitted on Sundays by permit whilst the sheds at Crewe North and South were normally closed to visitors or restricted to parties only. Writing to the Works for a permit every five or six weeks provided the necessary continuity for the out-shopping of locomotives. A charge of sixpence (2½p) in today's value) went to the St. Christopher Orphanage at Derby and later the Crewe Railway Charity Fund. I also joined the A.M.R. East Midlands Locospotters Club visiting Manchester District sheds and enjoyed a trip involving ex-LMS Compound No.1000.

A popular haunt where I spent many happy hours was Trent Lock; also referred to as 'Bunker' it was a busy location on a summer Sunday evening, (even more so in the week when freight trains were running) where, situated between Trent Junction signal box and Red Hill tunnel, it was an ideal spot, the only trains that did not pass that point were those running between Derby and Nottingham.

Conversely, during the week there was a considerable amount of freight traffic going onto and off the Castle Donington branch that would be missed. Equally, if train spotters positioned themselves in the vicinity of, or on Trent station, they would miss out on those St. Pancras-Manchester expresses streaking by half-a-mile away between Trent Junction and Sheet Stores Junction.

Crewe Locomotive Works 16th February 1964. BR Standard Class 9F 2-10-0 No. 92099 allocated to Tyne Dock (52H) and Stanier Class 5 No. 45045 amongst the locomotives outshopped.

1389

British Transport Commission.

British Railways,
Locomotive Works,
CREWE.

OFFICIAL PERMIT (JUVENILE 6d)

Admit one JUVENILE into the Works on
.... 15 DEC 1957 .... at 2.30pm.

(Proceeds for the Crewe Railway Charity Fund)

The first Midland Compound
No. 1000. Withdrawn in 1951
and stored at Crewe. The
engine was restored in 1959 at
Derby to a near original condition and placed in service on
enthusiast's specials. Is seen
here with a Stephenson Locomotive Society excursion
passing Lock Lane Crossing on
the Castle Donington branch
on a Sunday in 1959, diverted
because of engineering works
between Sawley Junction and
Derby.
J.A. Wade

Trent Lock often referred to as
'Bunker'. View from the down
main line of the viaducts over
the River Trent and Red Hill
tunnels taken on 26th July
1956.
Tony Smith

Interrupting the flow of the River Trent on its way out into the North Sea through the
East Midlands there were two weirs, within a mile of each other. The first was at nearby
Sawley just downstream from where the River Derwent had met the Trent, whilst the
other one was located near to Trent Lock a few yards further down from its meeting with
the River Soar. When this weir inextricably burst in 1953, it undermined the abutments
of the viaduct that carried the goods lines; boulders were then unloaded from rail vehicles to consolidate the footings.

The Central Electric Generating Boards power station at Ratcliffe-on-Soar, completed
in 1968 towers above Red Hill tunnel and can be seen for miles around, as can the
discharge it creates, a blot on the horizon many would say.

*   *   *

Quite unexpectedly in the mid 1950s, five ex-G.C.R. 'D11' Class 'Director' 4-4-0s allocated to the Eastern Region depot at Lincoln (40A) began to permeate the Midland

One of two photographs taken by Toton driver William Webb of the viaduct over the goods lines at Trent Lock in 1953 when the weir clearly visible inextricably broke. The milepost depicts 119 miles to St. Pancras.

Weirs were constructed downstream to protect the base of such bridges from the undermining effects of scour in the sometimes ferocious currents so that the water flowed more evenly around the piers, and at a relatively constant depth. Protected by a pile of boulders, the water, where it actually flowed around the base was slower and more tranquil than at the surface, and the piers were never undermined. Owing to the failure of the Midland weir; the River Trent was drained for several feet resulting in the ancient foundations being exposed for the first time since they were built.

lines. The former Midland shed at Lincoln had come under the control of the E.R. and although a small number of L.M. engines were still maintained there, most of the through workings between Lincoln and Derby were in the hands of Eastern Region locomotives. In the spring of 1957, five 'D16s' from Cambridge replaced the 'D11' engines, which were transferred to Sheffield Darnall (41A). That proved temporary, as a year later the 'D16s' were themselves replaced by the introduction of Diesel Multiple Units on the Derby to Lincoln, Leicester and Nottingham services. It was in April 1954 that the first lightweight diesel railcar emerged from the Litchurch Lane Works in Derby. Over the next five years 1,000 such vehicles would be turned out. A programme of driver training

(handling) was undertaken using the Churnet Valley branch line between Leek and Rocester finishing in the afternoon by the DMUs running via Chaddesden and the North Curve at Trent then back into Derby C & W Works.

*   *   *

During the dark winter nights, one of the porters at Draycott and Breaston station, George Mellors, would allow some of the lads access onto the premises to take engine numbers, illumination being provided by the strategically placed gas lights. His colleague, Granddad Ainsworth, (Grumpy), would have none of it and locked the large entrance gate to the station yard quite early. Waiting rooms at the smaller stations had an aura of their own, tobacco residue aside, the often-sparse decor with broad fixed benches and solitary gaslight illuminating the selection of handbills advertising forthcoming excursions. The small waiting room on the down side to Derby, with a central fireplace, contrasted with the more spacious one adjoining the booking office on the other platform, which was complete with wooden floors, and incorporated booking office, hall with a room leading off to a parcels area and cycle racks. The platform staff was alerted of the imminent arrival of a stopping train by two rings on the platform bell for a Nottingham train and three rings for a Derby bound service.

One afternoon, barely out of school, sitting as I had done for hours over the years astride the 'Shut and fasten gate', the 1.55 p.m. Derby-St. Pancras express hauled by a 'Jubilee' rushed past braking heavily. I had noticed that the distant signal, operated by the signalman at Sawley Crossing that was situated beneath the Draycott 'box starting signal

Just a little over three quarters of a mile from what was initially known as Breaston station, this is Draycott, renamed Draycott & Breaston in 1939 owing to the increase in housing locally. This 1958 picture looking towards Derby has an overbridge in the background which carried a major road and was about to be replaced by a new concrete structure. The station closed on 14th February 1966
J.A. Wade

had not been cleared. From my vantage point I could observe the level crossing gates at Sawley being closed to road traffic as the train approached them. The express came to a stand at Sawley Crossing, whether it had run by the home signal was conjecturable; it was a close run thing. Interestingly, some months later an outer distant signal was installed and situated underneath Draycott's home signal and motor operated. Seldom had I observed an express being checked on the up line, the almost 2½ miles distance between Borrowash and Draycott signal boxes usually provided the necessary headway. Conversely, on the down road signal checks did occur at Draycott whilst waiting for the previous train to have cleared Borrowash. Some years earlier, it had crossed my mind that I thought it a little unusual that on the opposite line there was inner and outer distant signals controlled from Draycott, whereas on the up line which was on a slightly falling gradient, Sawley Crossing only had one distant signal. The distance between the two signal boxes was 1339 yards, with some 900 yards (give or take a few) between the distant and home signal worked by Sawley Crossing.

*   *   *

Like so many other boys of my generation, I wanted to be an engine driver; two boys in my class had applied successfully for the position of engine cleaner at Toton Motive Power Depot. My dreams were dashed in 1956 when I went for a medical at Derby station. So much depended upon having perfect eyesight that I was extremely nervous. Fearful of failing, I became confused over white, yellow and orange colours flashed in different sequences, gradually getting smaller in size to simulate signals at various distances. The examination comprised tests for ordinary and colour vision. There was also an ingenious book designed by a Japanese professor called Ishiara. It contained various pages incorporating a number interposed in coloured dots, the number being identifiable by someone with normal colour vision. Those with defective vision may see different numbers or no number at all.

Remains of Sawley station closed in 1930, a Class 4F 0-6-0 is approaching with an eastbound freight in November 1957.
J.A. Wade

Forty-eight hours later my apprehension was realised. The caller-up from Toton was the bringer of bad news, opening the letter with trepidation, half expecting the worst.

```
                                        B.R. 14300/98
        4.   BRITISH   TRANSPORT   COMMISSION
R. J. POWELL
District Operating Superintendent
                                        DISTRICT OPERATING
Telephone                                 SUPERINTENDENT
NOTTINGHAM 85251                        LONDON MIDLAND REGION
Ext.                                           NOTTINGHAM
Telegraphic Address
DISTROP MIDLAND STATION
NOTTINGHAM

Our Reference
          S.3.           16th July, 1956.
Your Reference

Mr. R. H. Fowkes,
7 The Green,
Breaston,
Derby.

Dear Sir,

        With reference to your letter of the 14th instant,
whilst employed as a Junior Porter you would have ample
opportunity for preparing yourself for promotion on
attaining adult age to the positions of Signalman,
Goods Guard, Goods Shunter, etc.

        Evening classes are held at various points
during the winter months to enable staff to increase
their knowledge in the various phases of railway
operation.

        I enclose a folder for your information.

        I shall be to receive your application for
employment form duly completed at your early
convenience.

                        Yours faithfully,

                        for R.J. POWELL
```

I had not attained the required colour vision level and was therefore unsuitable for the footplate grade. It was truly the darkest period I had known; I probably wept at the time. The lifetime ambition to be an engine driver was over, I had failed at the first hurdle, and later it turned out to be all the more poignant that my two classmates, who had been successful in joining the footplate grade as cleaners left after only a short time. The consolation of being offered the position of Junior Porter, which at the time was not taken up, I don't recollect why, was of little consequence. Just what type of work did I now want? Still reeling from the disappointment of a lifelong desire to be an engine driver, I went to work for Jones & Strouds, an elasticated fabrics firm in Long Eaton.

A degree of solace was found in the visit to the station house at Upper Broughton on the Nottingham-Kettering line where my uncle and aunt lived. Situated not far from Melton Mowbray, the station lost its passenger service and was closed in 1948, but here I could contemplate my inner thoughts. The railway line was in a cutting, and being a Sunday trains were infrequent, Uncle George could never remember the times that they passed his house, by the time one was heard it had gone by when I got outside. Located a mile outside the village, the property had no electricity, gas and no flush toilet, cooking facilities might have appeared a little primitive but the dinner was always worthy of the journey, despite having to change bus stations in Nottingham. An old fashioned couple that rarely listened to the wireless, Uncle George actually played the violin and usually gave us a performance after dinner, in those days taken at lunchtimes.

Two

The Way In

After almost five months in the wilderness, help was at hand and it came by way of a porter at Draycott & Breaston station. I still had a yearning for the railway and kept in touch with happenings locally in the shape of wee George Mellors at the station. A likeable fellow, George rode the station bicycle in a very uncertain manner when he was delivering parcels between trains; he was also renowned for his rendering of 'Draycott' in his high-pitched falsetto voice when a train arrived at the station.

One day, he was showing me how to knock the crank of my bicycle back into shape (it had fallen over and as a result the crank was catching on the frame) when he mentioned that there was a vacancy at Trent for a Junior Porter, a position I had earlier turned down. This opportunity could not be allowed to pass; I applied for the job, I was successful and on 14th January 1957 I began my 39-year career with British Railways. Some years later I would work alongside George at Draycott & Breaston station on the odd occasions when requested to cover a vacancy for a porter, although at that time I was Telegraph and Booking Clerk at Trent.

Reproduced courtesy *Steam World* magazine

    *   *   *

"Well I'll go to Trent", was another expression my mother often used to make when faced with a situation surpassing belief. Trent, in the southeast corner of Derbyshire, was a station without a town, 119¾ miles from St. Pancras, on the Midland Lines of the London Midland Region. The River Trent, third longest river in England, from which it takes its name, runs nearby. The station, a sizeable one with the usual station buildings, only had a single island platform. It was opened in 1862 and surrounded only by an isolated farm and a cottage linked to the rifle range; there was also the stationmaster's house and ten railway cottages. With no buses passing the station entrance and no taxi rank,

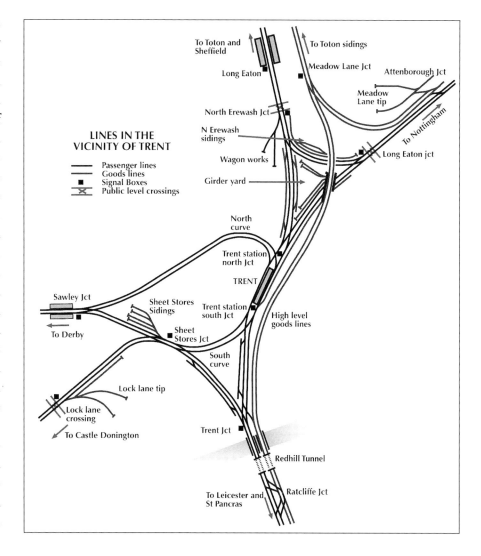

LINES IN THE VICINITY OF TRENT

——	Passenger lines
——	Goods lines
■	Signal Boxes
✕	Public level crossings

Coming off the goods line at Trent Station North Junction with the evening 6.28 p.m. Toton-Washwood Heath freight on 14th July 1959 is Class 4F 0-6-0 No. 43955. Some of the ten railway cottages are visible on the right.
Tony Smith

(Left) A Leeds District LMS Class 8F 2-8-0 No. 48274 ambles through Trent station with a down freight in August 1952.
J.A. Wade

(Right) Derailed engine and tender of Class 3F 0-6-0 No. 43650 at the entrance to the works of Messrs. Wagon Repairs Long Eaton. In doing so it has blocked the footpath that ran from North Erewash Junction signalbox (in the background) to Trent station.
J.A. Wade

many would-be passengers opted for Shank's pony as a means of getting to the station, either by using the 600 yard sparsely gas lit footpath from North Erewash Junction or by the longer route down Meadow Lane and over Long Eaton Junction level crossing.

* * *

At the turn of the century there were two identical rows of trees on either side of the platform (see opposite, top left), those on the north side are still evident, whilst those on the south side were felled to facilitate the building of the high-level goods lines into Toton. This allowed the intensive workings, which carried the heaviest freight traffic in the country to avoid Trent station and also the two busy level crossings in later years in Long Eaton. Over the years Trent won many awards, in 1953 a first prize for cleanliness and a

third for its gardens. Although not widely known, all manner of Royalty visited Trent, albeit in the form of the Royal train that was stabled overnight on the North Curve between Trent Station North Junction and Sawley Junction. Other well-known celebrities would change trains at Trent; amongst those mentioned to me by George Bailey was Ella Fitzgerald and on one occasion I saw Primo Carnera on the platform.

Trent station was last century some might say, one of the cornerstones of the Midland Railway Empire. Of Midland Gothic architecture with its honeycomb of cellars and inter-linking upper storeys, Trent's position and importance as an interchange junction for five main railway routes, through the plethora of junctions, served London, Birmingham, Derby, Chesterfield and Nottingham. Remarkably enough, trains could depart from opposite platforms in opposite directions to the same destination.

When I reported to A.W. (Tony) Smith the stationmaster, on the first day, he explained the role of a Junior Porter as a general-purpose relief, with a rate of pay 63 shillings (£3.15p on today's value) per week. I was to relieve the control reporters – signal box lads – at Sheet Stores Junction, Trent Station South Junction, Toton Centre, Stanton Gate North Junction, Ilkeston South Junction and Beeston North. For whatever reason and I know not why,

(Left) Hughes-Fowler rated 6P5F 2-6-0 No. 42769 often referred to as a 'Crab' ambles along the 3rd down passenger line at Trent with a train of empty wagons for Beeston sidings. Initially there were lines of trees on either side of the station, those on the up side being felled to facilitate the building of the high level goods lines into Toton Yard.

(Right) Midland 4-4-0 (3-Cyl. Compound.) Class 4P No. 40929 leaving Trent station with the 11. 5 a.m. Nottingham-Derby local train on 31st August 1956. The next lines are the 2nd up passenger then the 3rd up passenger and the goods line from Long Eaton Junction to Trent Station South Junction, (Trent Station North 'box not involved with that line). On the extreme right are the high-level goods lines to and from Toton. *Tony Smith*

(Middle) LMS Class 8F 2-8-0 No. 48206 getting into its stride at North Erewash Junction after negotiating the second of two level crossings since leaving Toton with a mineral train for Washwood Heath in April 1955. *J.A. Wade*

(Bottom) Stanier Class 8F 2-8-0 No. 48620 waits on the up goods line at Trent Station South Junction with a freight from Beeston to follow the DMU leaving the platform on 14th May 1959. *Tony Smith*

sometime much later I expressed a wish not to relieve at Beeston North; it had nothing to do with the mileage involved as Ilkeston was roughly the same distance from my home. I did, however, have a spell at Beeston station assisting in the seasonal despatch of hundreds of rose trees from the nearby Gregory nursery. The trees came packed in straw, all sizes, each one having a centre number appended before being loaded into whatever brakevan space was available. Fortunately this duty was only temporary and I returned to box lad duties. As Trent was my home station, time spent travelling to the outlying signal boxes would equate to a walking time of 20 minutes to the mile, unless a train

TRENT STATION TRAIN WORKING 1961		
TRAIN	**ARR DEP**	**DESTINATION**
23.55 NOTTINGHAM	00.09 00.11	DERBY
01.32 DERBY	01.47 01.49	NOTTINGHAM
23.50 ST.PANCRAS	03.01 03.03	LEEDS CITY
02.25 TAMWORTH	03.33 03.35	LINCOLN
06.00 NOTTINGHAM	06.14 06.16	LEICESTER
06.25 NOTTINGHAM	06.44 06.50	DERBY
06.30 DERBY	06.50 06.51	NOTTINGHAM
06.40 NOTTINGHAM	06.55 06.57	ST.PANCRAS
06.10 LEICESTER	07.08 07.10	NOTTINGHAM
07.00 DERBY	07.20 07.21	LINCOLN
07.16 NOTTINGHAM	07.33 07.34	LEICESTER
07.35 DERBY	08.00 08.02	NOTTINGHAM
07.44 NOTTINGHAM	08.01 08.02	DERBY
07.38 LEICESTER	08.15 08.16	NOTTINGHAM
07.05 LINCOLN	08.27 08.27	DERBY
08.16 DERBY	08.36 08.37	LINCOLN
08.33 NOTTINGHAM	08.46 08.46	BIRMINGHAM
08.35 LEICESTER	09.08 0910	NOTTINGHAM
09.00 NOTTINGHAM	09.14 09.17	MANCHESTER CEN
08.10 LINCOLN	09.23 09.23	DERBY
09.20 DERBY	09.40 09.40	LINCOLN
09.30 NOTTINGHAM	09.41 09.41	BIRMINGHAM
08.25 BIRMINGHAM	10.01 10.03	NOTTINGHAM
09.10 LINCOLN	10.23 10.23	DERBY
09.55 LEICESTER	10.25 10.27	NOTTINGHAM
10.20 DERBY	10.40 10.40	LINCOLN
10.30 NOTTINGHAM	10.43 10.43	BIRMINGHAM
10.40 NOTTINGHAM	10.50 10.50	DERBY
10.53 DERBY	11.07 11.07	NOTTINGHAM
10.55 NOTTINGHAM	11.08 11.08	LEICESTER
09.15 BIRMINGHAM	11.16 11.18	NOTTINGHAM
11.20 DERBY	11.40 11.40	LINCOLN
10.10 LINCOLN	11.43 11.43	DERBY
10.15 BIRMINGHAM	12.11 12.11	NOTTINGHAM
12.00 NOTTINGHAM	12.14 12.16	ST.PANCRAS
11.10 LINCOLN	12.28 12.28	DERBY
12.20 DERBY	12.40 12.41	LINCOLN
12.40 NOTTINGHAM	12.53 12.53	BIRMINGHAM
12.40 LEICESTER	13.16 13.18	NOTTINGHAM
12.10 LINCOLN	13.24 13.25	DERBY
13.20 DERBY	13.40 13.40	LINCOLN

13.35 NOTTINGHAM	13.48 13.48	BIRMINGHAM
12.15 BIRMINGHAM	14.16 14.16	NOTTINGHAM
12.15 ST.PANCRAS	14.23 14.25	BRADFORD F SQ
13.10 LINCOLN	14.23 14.29	DERBY
14.23 DERBY	14.41 14.41	LINCOLN
12.25 ST.PANCRAS	14.48 14.50	MANCHESTER CEN
14.45 NOTTINGHAM	14.58 14.58	BIRMINGHAM
13.15 BIRMINGHAM	15.16 15.16	NOTTINGHAM
14.10 LINCOLN	15.26 15.26	DERBY
15.20 DERBY	15.40 15.40	LINCOLN
15.30 NOTTINGHAM	15.43 15.43	BIRMINGHAM
15.25 LEICESTER	15.58 16.00	NOTTINGHAM
16.04 NOTTINGHAM	16.15 16.16	DERBY
09.20 GLASGOW ST.E	16.44 16.45	ST.PANCRAS
16.25 DERBY	16.47 16.48	LINCOLN
16.35 NOTTINGHAM	16.48 16.50	BIRMINGHAM
15.15 BIRMINGHAM	17.06 17.09	NOTTINGHAM
16.54 NOTTINGHAM	17.11 17.13	DERBY
17.08 NOTTINGHAM	17.25 17.26	LEICESTER
17.08 DERBY	17.32 17.33	NOTTINGHAM
16.10 LINCOLN	17.34 17.34	DERBY
17.30 NOTTINGHAM	17.43 17.43	BIRMINGHAM
15.25 MANCHESTER	17.50 17.51	NOTTINGHAM
17.10 LEICESTER	17.56 17.58	NOTTINGHAM
17.45 DERBY	18.10 18.12	NOTTINGHAM
17.40 LEICESTER	18.16 18.20	NOTTINGHAM
17.10 LINCOLN	18.23 18.23	DERBY
17.05 BIRMINGHAM	18.27 18.29	NOTTINGHAM
18.20 DERBY	18.40 18.42	LINCOLN
18.30 NOTTINGHAM	18.43 18.43	BIRMINGHAM
17.15 BIRMINGHAM	19.04 19.05	NOTTINGHAM
18.10 LINCOLN	19.23 19.23	DERBY
19.25 DERBY	19.43 19.46	LINCOLN
19.30 NOTTINGHAM	19.45 19.45	LEICESTER
19.38 LEICESTER	20.20 20.22	NOTTINGHAM
19.10 LINCOLN	20.23 20.23	DERBY
20.33 DERBY	20.55 20.56	LINCOLN
20.43 NOTTINGHAM	20.56 20.57	LEICESTER
19.57 LINCOLN	21.17 21.19	TAMWORTH
19.15 BIRMINGHAM	21.30 21.30	NOTTINGHAM
20.20 LINCOLN	21.35 21.35	DERBY
21.20 DERBY	21.40 21.41	LINCOLN
21.55 NOTTINGHAM	22.12 22.13	LEICESTER
21.10 LINCOLN	22.23 22.23	DERBY
22.20 DERBY	22.38 22.39	NOTTINGHAM
22.30 NOTTINGHAM	22.49 22.50	LEICESTER
22.20 LEICESTER	23.03 23.05	NOTTINGHAM
22.50 NOTTINGHAM	23.07 23.15	DERBY

service was available. It was extremely remunerative to relieve at Ilkeston South Junction on the early turn, realising an extra 4½ hours pay.

*   *   *

With my training at the signal boxes completed and with no control reporting duties to undertake, I reverted to Junior Porter's duties at Trent station. In its heyday Trent was one of the most important junctions on the Midland lines with very few trains not stopping there. During each 24 hours nearly 100 passenger and parcels trains called at Trent; in those days they were mainly locomotive-hauled coaching stock including archaic non-

DIESEL SERVICES   **BRITISH RAILWAYS**

NOTTINGHAM MIDLAND
DERBY MIDLAND

10th September 1962 to 16th June 1963 or until further notice

For full services between Leicester and Trent see folder AD7

A05

DERBY MIDLAND — NOTTINGHAM MIDLAND

WEEKDAYS

(dense timetable of train departure/arrival times for Derby Midland, Spondon, Borrowash, Draycott and Breaston, Sawley Junction (for Long Eaton), Trent, Trent dep. for Leicester, Leicester London Road, Attenborough, Beeston, Nottingham Midland)

WEEKDAYS — continued

(continuation of timetable)

SUNDAYS

(Sunday timetable)

A—Through train to Lincoln.   B—Through train from Leicester.   D—Diesel train.   E—Runs from 28th October 1962 until 7th April 1963.
F—Runs until 21st October 1962 and from 14th April 1963
MO—Mondays only.   MX—Mondays excepted.   SO—Saturdays only.   SX—Saturdays excepted.   h—Applies from 14th April 1963.
TRAINS NOT INDICATED BY "D" ARE STEAM TRAINS.   THESE SERVICES ARE SUBJECT TO ALTERATION

NOTTINGHAM MIDLAND — DERBY MIDLAND

WEEKDAYS

(dense timetable of train departure/arrival times for Nottingham Midland, Beeston, Attenborough, Trent, Leicester London Road, Trent arr. from Leicester, Trent, Sawley Junction (for Long Eaton), Draycott and Breaston, Borrowash, Spondon, Derby Midland)

WEEKDAYS — continued

(continuation of timetable)

SUNDAYS

(Sunday timetable)

A—Through train from Lincoln.   B—Through train to Leicester.   D—Diesel train.   FO—Fridays only.
SO—Saturdays only.   x or SX—Saturdays excepted.   MWFO—Mondays, Wednesdays, Fridays only.
h—Applies from 14th April 1963
TRAINS NOT INDICATED BY "D" ARE STEAM TRAINS.   THESE SERVICES ARE SUBJECT TO ALTERATION.

DIESEL SERVICES   **BRITISH RAILWAYS**

LEICESTER LONDON ROAD
NOTTINGHAM MIDLAND

Also Passenger Train Services

LEICESTER CENTRAL
NOTTINGHAM VICTORIA

10th September, 1962 to 16th June, 1963
For full services between Nottingham Midland and Trent see folder AD8

AD7
Williams (Midland) Ltd., Market

LEICESTER LONDON ROAD—NOTTINGHAM MIDLAND

WEEKDAYS

(dense timetable for Leicester London Road, Humberstone Road, Syston, Sileby, Barrow-on-Soar, Loughborough Midland, Kegworth, Trent, Trent dep. for Derby Midland, Derby Midland, Trent, Attenborough, Beeston, Nottingham Midland)

WEEKDAYS — continued

(continuation of timetable)

SUNDAYS

(Sunday timetable)

a—Applies from 14th April, 1963.   B—Through train to Derby.   D—Diesel train.   e—Change at Trent.   MO—Mondays only.   SO—Saturdays only.   SX—Saturdays excepted.
TRAINS NOT INDICATED BY "D" ARE STEAM TRAINS.   These services are subject to alteration.   T—Through train from Birmingham New St.
P. Midland Pullman.   First Class only.   Supplementary charge payable in addition to First Class fare.   Does not run 24, 25, 26 & 31 December, 1962, 1st January, 11th, 12th & 15th April, 31 May & 3rd June, 1963

NOTTINGHAM MIDLAND—LEICESTER LONDON ROAD

WEEKDAYS

		MO am	B am	B am	D am		am	am	D am	am	am	TD am	B am	am	am	am	B am	TD am		TD am	SX B am	TD am	B am		am				SO pm	SO TD pm	pm		DT pm
NOTTINGHAM MIDLAND	dep.	12 58			6 55				7 30				8 30				9 30			10 30		11 30		11 55					12 30		1 30	
Beeston				6 00	7 01				7 35				8 35				9 35			10 35		11 35		12 01					12 35		1 35	
Attenborough				6 07	6e37				7 39				8 39				9 39			10 39		11 39							12 39		1 39	
Trent	arr.			6 14	7 08				7 44				8 44				9 44			10 44		11 44		12 08					12 44		1 44	
Derby Midland	dep.		1 05	2 05	6 32			7 10	8 00	#05	8 15		9 03	9 20	10 4	10 20	10 55	11 20	11 54			12 20		1 20	
Trent arr. from Derby Midland					6 52			7 31			8 37		9 41		10 41							
Trent	dep.				6 16	7 09			7 44			8 44		9 44		10 44		11 44		12 10			12 44		1 44
Kegworth			1 28		6 23		7 20	7 27	7 50		8 23	8 50	9 23	9 50		10 50		11 50				12 50		1 50
Loughborough Midland					6 33			7 32	7 57		8 30	8 57		9 57		10 57		11 57	12 21			12 57		1 57
Barrow-on-Soar					6 39			7 37	8 02			9 02		10 02		11 02		12 02				1 02		2 02
Sileby					6 44				8 07			9 06		10 06		11 06		12 06				1 07		2 06
Syston					6 49		7 42	8 01	8 12			9 11	9 26	10 11		11 11		12 11				1 12	1 44	2 11
Humberstone Road					6 56		7 49	8 08	8 18					1sx17						1 51
LEICESTER LONDON ROAD	arr.	1 32	1 46	2 42	7 00	7 37	7 53	8 12	8 21	8 33	8 47	9 21	9 34	9 40	10 19	10 37	11 28	12 19	12 27	12 38		12 50	1 20	1 53	2 19

WEEKDAYS—continued

		B pm	pm	pm	SO TD pm	pm	SX P pm	pm	B pm	TD pm	TD pm	pm	pm	D pm	pm	pm	SX D pm	pm	pm	pm	TD pm	B pm	pm	pm	SO TD pm	pm	pm	pm	pm	D pm	B pm	pm	pm	D pm
NOTTINGHAM MIDLAND	dep.			2e10	2 40		3 30			3 42	4 39			5 08		5 30			6 30			7 30			9 55	
Beeston				2e15	2 45				3 47	4 44			5 14		5 35			6 35			7 35			10 01	
Attenborough				2e19	2 49				3 51	4 44!			5 18		5 39			6 39			7 39			10 04	
Trent	arr.			2 24	2 54				3 56	4 49			5 24		5 44			6 44			7 44			10 09	
Derby Midland	dep.	1 50			2 20				3 25		4 25		5 5		5 10	5 45			7 20	7 45		9 20	
Trent arr. from Derby Midland				2 41			3 46		4 48!			5 34			7 41		9 41	
Trent	dep.		2 34	2 54			3 53	56	4 49			5 24	5 44		6 44		7 44			10 09
Kegworth				3 0				4 2	4 54			5 31	5 50		6 50		7 50			10 16
Loughborough Midland				3 06			3 47	4 9	5 07		5 30	5 40	5 57	6 07	6 56		7 57	8 08		10 24
Barrow-on-Soar				3 11				4 15	5 12			5 46	6 02		7 02		8 02			10 30
Sileby				3 16				4 19	5 16			5 51	6 06		7 06		8 06			10 35
Syston				3 14	3 21			4 24	5 20	5 5	14	6 11	6 35	7 11		8 11		10 04	10 40
Humberstone Road								5sx21	5sx22		6sx5	6sx43						
LEICESTER LONDON ROAD	arr.	2 33	2 57	3 23	3 29		4 00	4 16	4 32	5 32	5 25	5 47	6 8	6 19	6 24	6 47	7 19		7 31	8 19	8 24	10 13	10 49

SUNDAYS

		B am		B am		am	am	D am	am	am	B am	am	TD am		D pm	pm	pm	pm	D pm	B pm	B pm	TD pm	B pm	B pm	D pm	B pm		D pm	pm	pm	D pm	B pm
NOTTINGHAM MIDLAND	dep.					8 35	9 40			11 40			2 00			3 40			5 15		7 0			7 52			9 40	10e45
Beeston						8 41	9 45			11 45			2 05			3 45			5 20		7 5			7 57			9 45	10e50
Attenborough							9e49			11a49			2a09			3a49			5a24								9a49	10ae54
Trent	arr.					8 48	9 54			11 54			2 14			3 54			5 29		7 12			8 4			9 54	10 59
Derby Midland	dep.	1 5		4 50		8 30		10 50		12 12	1 40		2 25		4 00	4 10		5 45	6 8		7 15		7 40	8 15		9 30	11 20
Trent arr. from Derby Midland					8 47				1 47						7 57			9 47	11 36
Trent	dep.	1 24				8 50	9 54		11 54		2 14			3 54			5 29		7 12		8 4		9 54	11 38
Kegworth						8 56	10 00		12 00		2 20						5 35		7 18		8 10		10 00
Loughborough Midland						9 03	10 07		12 07	12 44	2 27		4 07		4 31	5 42		7 25	7 37		8 17	8 37		10 07	11 50
Barrow-on-Soar						9 10	10 16		12 12		2 36		4 12			5 47		7 30		8 22		10 12
Sileby						9 14	10 16		12 16		2 36		4 16			5 51		7 35		8 27		10 16
Syston						9 19	10 21	10 41	12 21		2 41	2 49	4 21			5 57		7 40		8 32	9 07	10 21	am
LEICESTER LONDON ROAD	arr.	1 54		5 24		9 26	10 29	10 50	11 26	12 50	11 31	3 06	4 39	4 36	4 51	6 05	6 19	6 45	7 48	7 54	8 05	8 40	8 54	9 16	10 29	12 08

a—Applies from 14th April, 1963.   B—Through train from Derby.   e—Change at Trent.   D—Diesel train.   MO—Mondays only.   SO—Saturdays only.
SX—Saturdays excepted.   TRAINS NOT INDICATED BY 'D' ARE STEAM TRAINS.   These services are subject to alteration.   T—Through Train to Birmingham New St.
P. Midland Pullman.   First Class only.   Supplementary charge payable in addition to First Class Fare.   Does not run 24, 25, 26 & 31 December, 1962, 1st January, 11, 12, & 15 April, 31st May & 1st June, 1963

corridor coaches on workmen's services, these eventually giving way to diesel multiple-units running between Derby, Nottingham & Lincoln, Leicester and Birmingham. The two routes connected at Trent to provide an interval service between Derby and Leicester that supplemented the Manchester to St. Pancras expresses. One of the biggest problems at the station was whether to hold the trains for connection in the event of late running, bearing in mind that a connection maintained at Trent may result in another being missed elsewhere. The Divisional Manager, Nottingham, issued guidelines, in the form of 'Detention of Trains for Connection at Trent'.

As a relief control reporter who went to signal boxes on an irregular basis, it was often difficult to be on the same wavelength as the signalmen. This obviously worked both ways. On the odd occasions when I was at Ilkeston South Junction, it was a pleasure working with Arthur Cox who, knowing my interest in gardening, told me that if potatoes were earthed up when planted it would produce a higher yield. His colleague Walter was heavily into the ministerial scene, I recall.

It was on the down No.2 goods line between Trowell Junction and Ilkeston South Junction during the early 1950s that Westinghouse Brake Trials were conducted with empty 16-ton fitted mineral wagons, these trials also ran from Toton to Bedford.

TO.........................

....

From: Divisional Manager,
Furlong House,
Middle Furlong Road,
NOTTINGHAM.

Ref: Q.24.
Extn: 057-2237
Date: April, 1967.

DETENTION OF TRAINS FOR CONNECTION AT TRENT.

No train may be delayed at Trent, for the purpose of making connection, except the following, which may be held for the length of time shown beyond the Working Book departure time, if by so doing, the advertised connections named below can be maintained.

A train which is already running late, may be held for only the additional time shown after its booked departure and not for that time after it is actually ready to leave.

These margins are intended to apply when the only work to be done is the usual transfer of passengers from one train to another. In cases where the transfer of loaded through vehicles has been pre-arranged, authority must be sought from the Control before exceeding the margin.

In the case of train marked ✱, if the marginal allowance shown will not enable the connection to be made, the Control must be consulted and will decide whether the train should be held for a longer period or despatched at its booked time and other arrangements be made.

My Control will instruct the S.M. what steps are to be taken if the connections are severed.

R.D. Gardiner

DETENTION OF TRAINS FOR CONNECTION

Train to	Due to depart	May be held after due departure time		For trains from	Due to arrive
DERBY	07.19	Not to be delayed		06.10 LEICESTER	07.02
BIRMINGHAM	07.34	5 Minutes		06.55 DERBY	07.12
DERBY	08.32	3 Minutes		06.40 WELLINGBORO	08.17
LEICESTER	08.37	Only if signalled		08.15 DERBY	08.31
DERBY	08.59	3 Minutes		08.18 LEICESTER	08.53
LEICESTER	16.47	5 Minutes		16.22 DERBY	16.39
DERBY	17.30	3 Minutes		16.40 LEICESTER	17.16
BIRMINGHAM	17.39	Only if signalled		17.10 DERBY	17.28
DERBY	18.03	5 Minutes		17.25 LEICESTER	18.02
DERBY	20.24	3 Minutes	✱	19.45 LEICESTER	20.20
LEICESTER	22.10 SX	5 Minutes	✱	21.45 DERBY	22.05½
LEICESTER	22.55 SO	5 Minutes	✱	22.25 DERBY	22.45
SUNDAYS					
DERBY	14.47	5 Minutes	✱	14.05 LEICESTER	14.41
BIRMINGHAM	16.17	5 Minutes		15.50 DERBY	16.05
DERBY	19.39	3 Minutes		19.00 LEICESTER	19.35
LEICESTER	20.23	5 Minutes	✱	19.50 DERBY	20.05
DERBY	22.02	5 Minutes	✱	21.00 LEICESTER	21.50
LEICESTER	22.12	5 Minutes	✱	21.50 DERBY	22.05

(Left) Just arriving at Trent station (signals still in the clear position at Trent Station North 'box) is another Midland 4-4-0 (3-Cyl. Compound.) Class 4P No. 41185 on 11th July 1956.

(Right) Appears to be leaking like a sieve, Midland 4-4-0 (3-Cyl. Compound.) Class 4P No. 41095 restarts the 8.7 a.m. Derby-Nottingham stopping train from Trent station on 3rd July 1956.

In addition, the Toton-Brent fully fitted test trains sported a variety of express motive power – 'Britannias', 'Royal Scots', 'Jubilees', Stanier Class '5' and BR Standard Class '5' locomotives.

Stanton Gate North Junction, with its token machine for the Old Works branch, is also well remembered. The collieries at Mapperley and Shipley together with the open-cast working at West Hallam also used the branch, as did traffic for the BSC ironworks, Stanton and Staveley being renowned overseas for their hardware.

On one occasion, there was an altercation between one of the signalmen and the foreman in the yard, very nearly a case of pistols at dawn. It had been simmering for a while; nevertheless it was interesting to say the least. Later I believe the signalman concerned left the service.

The 3.40 p.m. Derby-Lincoln passenger train was always worked by a 2-6-4 Tank engine running bunker first, returning later in the evening (chimney first) with the Lincoln-Tamworth mail. Pictured here is the 7.38 a.m. Leicester-Nottingham local train with a 2-6-4T engine leaving Trent station on 3rd July 1956.
Tony Smith

*   *   *

Not all control reporters of course were lads, some found there way into the signal box classed as 'green card' men, who owing to their condition could not undertake normal duties. Trent Station South Junction boasted a couple of these moaners, and my good-ness didn't the respective signalmen who had them as there regular mates look forward to their own and the moaners' rest days. Norman Dean was fortunate; he had a young lad

Passing Trent Station North Junction signalbox and entering Trent station is Fowler 2-6-4T No. 42330 with a Nottingham-Leicester local in July 1955.
J.A. Wade

In 1952 Westinghouse brake trials were carried out between Trowell Junction and Ilkeston Junction on the Erewash Valley. BR Standard Class 5 4-6-0 No. 73031 was fitted with air-pumps.

A relaxed fireman having a break on BR Standard Class 5 4-6-0 No. 73031 at Ilkeston South Junction 1952 during the Westinghouse brake trials.

Tony Martin as his mate. Poor Jack Constable and Sid Madeley had Bert Banks and Harry (bad legs) Hearn to contend with. Sid, to get away, moved to Toton Down Sidings North (shed box), while dear old Jack retired and later Norman moved to Mansfield Junction signal box at Nottingham. It would be true to say that most of the control reporters with possibly the exception of the green card men (some of whom might still have operated the block bells and instruments) did, unofficially of course work the signal boxes.

If the signalman was not careful he could create an impasse at Trent Station South Junction; unlikely as this may seem, it actu-

The interior of Trent Station South Junction signalbox taken on 25th July 1956. With signalman Norman Dean, in the centre, control reporter Tony Martin with A N Other on the telephone. It would be another five months before I joined the railway.
Tony Smith

(Right) Trent Station North Junction and signalman Albert Jones. 25th July 1956.
Tony Smith

ally happened although not through any lack of co-operation between the signalmen. A freight train for the Castle Donington branch had been accepted from Trent Station North Junction; the signalman at Trent South had a freight signalled for Toton coming from Trent Junction and it was routed along the platform line to Trent North. All very well, but when this train arrived at Trent North it was found to have been wrongly described, it was not for Toton and should have gone to Beeston. As a result of this direction error, we now had both trains unable to move forward along the proper route. One or other would have to advance a sufficient distance to allow the other train to pass and then to reverse, a time-consuming exercise with possibly sixty or so wagons in tow.

A spell at Toton Centre signal box covering a vacancy was, to say the least, interesting beyond belief. With contra-rotating shifts between signalmen and control reporters, one either loathed working with the redoubtable Bill Butler or, strangely enough, enjoyed it. Perhaps one week in three was sufficient, for at times working alongside him resembled something more akin to a pantomime.

The interior view, taken at Trent Station South Junction signalbox in 1957, shows signalman Norman Dean and Roderick H. Fowkes, box lad (control reporter).

The interior of Trent Station North Junction signalbox with signalman George Bailey. George was a signalman at Sheet Stores Junction before moving to Toton Centre (where I was his box lad for a spell) and then to Trent North and Sandiacre when the Power Box was commissioned

Bill could be a cantankerous individual and had a love/hate relationship with quite a few drivers. He liked nothing better than sliding open a window and thrusting a red light to stop a light-engine movement proceeding across the road if the locomotive was displaying incorrect headlights. After trains arrived on the Up reception roads on the New Bank, the locomotive would be released and then run light to the depot or to the North Yard or Meadow for its return working. These movements involved reversing across the main lines and some firemen could not be bothered to change over the lights. Some enginemen, knowing who was on duty, did this to annoy Bill and generally it was a war of words between the two factions. On one occasion, veiled threats were directed at the signalman after he tore down the steps to remonstrate with the footplate crew, the heated argument lasting minutes. The engine was straddling the crossover road, preventing the acceptance under normal conditions of trains on the main lines. Bill's father had also been a signalman and was reputed to have been an obstreperous person. The following week would see a return to more tranquil surroundings with either Jimmy Trigger or the placid George Bailey, who would later move to Trent Station North Junction, in charge of the signalbox at Toton Centre. Geoff Wall, a regular box lad, was always relieved when his week with Bill Butler was over.

There was extremely little train regulating to do at Toton Centre; engines to and from the depot and from yard to yard were about the sum total. The recording only entailed maintaining the train register book and there was no reporting at all to the Nottingham Control Office. On the other hand, it was a first class working environment – good access, brick-built with electricity, central heating, integral flush toilet and the company of the Old Bank shunter, whose leg Bill Butler used to pull unmercifully, referring to him as Inspector, Stan Salmon.

*   *   *

On the Midland Division of the London Midland Region, 'Jubilee' Class 4-6-0 locomotives, supplemented by Stanier Class '5's provided staple motive power for the expresses to and from St. Pancras. A feature of the Midland Division operation was the increase of much double heading, where, south of Derby and Nottingham, pre-war speeds had been fully restored, but with increased loads. A limit of 300 tons tare weight was fixed for a 'Jubilee' Class 4-6-0 on 'XL Limit' timings. Unfortunately, a nine-coach train of standard

One of the very few passenger trains that didn't call at Trent station. Routed through the 3rd up passenger line, 'Jubilee' Class 6P 4-6-0 No. 45654 'Hood' accelerating away with the 8.30 a.m. Sheffield- St. Pancras on 6th July 1959 whilst a freight from Beeston stands on the goods line awaiting a path.
Tony Smith

The introduction of six "Royal Scot" locos in 1957 and allocated to Kentish Town effectively reduced the uneconomic double heading on the Midland Lines. No. 46152 'Kings Dragoon Rifleman' has just passed Sheet Stores Junction with a Manchester Central-St. Pancras express in January 1958.
J.A. Wade

stock, including a restaurant car, exceeded this figure, so that a pilot could be called for by the driver of a 'Jubilee' as well as a Class '5' if he was expected to keep time on this schedule. With a 4-4-0 Class '2' or '4P' as the pilot engine, one did wonder at times whether this proved a hindrance or help. In 1955 'Royal Scot' No. 46120 'Royal Iniskilling Fusilier' had been on loan for twelve weeks to the M&EE department at Derby, chief duties being the 7.55 a.m. Derby to St. Pancras and the 5.30 p.m. St. Pancras to Nottingham. This may well have been the prelude to the transfer of six 'Royal Scots' from the Western Division sheds for the 1957 winter timetable. Allocated to Kentish Town Nos. 46110/6/27/31/52/57 initially confined their activities to the Manchester route, on 'XL Limit' schedules 300 tons being the allowance between Derby and Manchester whilst 340 tons applied elsewhere. This effectively reduced the uneconomic double heading.

A vacancy had now occurred at Sheet Stores Junction, which produced a lot of soul-searching whether or not to apply for the post. Toton Centre was fun and my week working alongside Bill Butler was always eagerly awaited, and then there were the relief signalmen, Les Robson and Ernie Mee, both of whom I had worked with at Trent Station South Junction; neither of them relieved the signalmen at Sheet Stores. So it was with a degree of sadness that I decided to move to the vacancy at Sheet Stores Junction, from there I would be reporting to the Control offices at both Derby and Nottingham with the regulating of trains also a primary attraction. On 13th January 1958, almost a year to the day from when I started on the railway, I transferred, forfeiting the weekly GPR allowance of 3 shillings (15p) a week. The days I spent on relief had been enjoyable even the galling

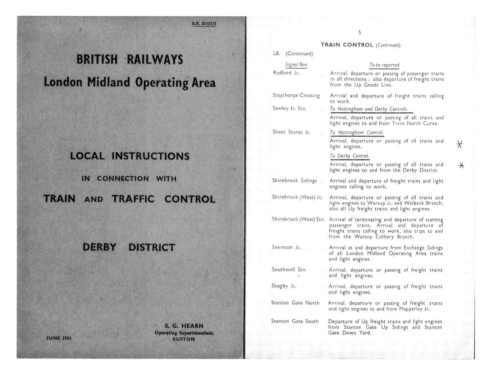

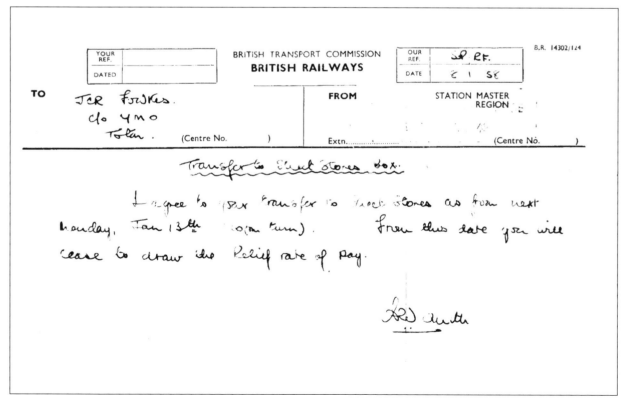

six or so mile cycle trek to Ilkeston for a 6 a.m. start was now at an end. There was still the opportunity to keep in touch both in person and by telephone, with some of the signalmen with whom I worked. Others, however, would become a distant memory.

* * *

Sheet Stores Junction Signal Box was normally accessible from three sides, by cycle or on foot along the cess from Trent station, along the tarmac footpath from Sawley Junction over the canal, dropping steeply down through a tunnel under the railway to the cycle shed. Care had to be taken negotiating this short tunnel as there were steel running tracks used for the internal movement of trucks from the various buildings. The other access point was off the Tamworth Road alongside the canal. This was just wide enough for a motor vehicle although then, most relied on pedal power.

An unidentified LMS Class 8F 2-8-0 has a clear road onto the branch with a Toton-Washwood Heath freight, circa 1959. Part of the Sheet Stores factory, from which the junction took its name is visible on the down side.

The Midland was a railway of distinction. Its signal boxes were of wooden construction, the lower half up to floor level finished in overlapping horizontal boarding, painted, in banana yellow with plum ends and surrounds. The large window frames were white, some opening whilst others were fixed. Identification of the signal box in my time was by means of a nameboard at either end.

A railed gallery for window cleaning was provided round the front and side of most signal boxes. Inside, the linoleum floor was washed weekly and newspapers were placed down to protect the surface; some floors were also polished. A wooden horizontal locker, comprising three separate lockers, one for each of the regular signalmen, together with a spare, usually had a board at one end which, when adjusted, provided a relaxing posture for the occupant when not working. The board was usually located adjacent to the omnibus telephone circuits, where, each morning, a roll call – a series of intermittent short rings heralded the time check for 9 a.m.

The most distinctive feature was the lever frame itself. Instead of the bare levers coming up through the floor, the lower ends were encased within a cover about two feet high running the length of the frame, together with a two inch thick wooden plank

roughly a foot wide at floor level. This was useful in providing leverage when operating points and pulling distant signals off, with the added help of a foot up on the frame.

The frame casing carried a series of engraved brass plates with the lever descriptions; the lever also had a small brass plate on the front giving its number and the numbers of the levers that had to be pulled first to free it. A duster was often regarded by some railway writers as being part of the basic equipment, which the signalman would place over the top of the lever when operating it. In my experience not many signalmen bothered using a duster.

A shelf for the signalling apparatus was suspended over the lever frame. On it were the block instruments, bells and other equipment, signal repeaters, box-to-box telephone and signal light indicators. Each bell had a distinctive tone; a central stem into a mahogany box, which housed an electromagnet operating the bell tapper, held the bell dome. Deft light fingering was all that was required and the bell would ring in the next box. If treated with a heavy hand, only a click would be produced. Some bells were extremely loud, shades of Big Ben, but wedging a piece of wood between the bell dome and the mechanism box quietened others down. Some relief signalmen, who had not worked a particular box for some months, were often

Sheet Stores Junction signalbox, where I worked, was a standard Midland Railway design. This view is looking southeast and LMS '8F' 2-8-0 N0. 48646 is working a Beeston-Chaddesden freight on 15th July 1964 on the South curve from Trent station. The line to the right is from Leicester.

Easter Region B1 Class 4-6-0 No. 61258 passing Sheet Stores Junction signalbox with a Derby-Lincoln stopping train in December 1957. I could well have been on duty in the 'box as control reporter.
J.A. Wade

Heading south at Sheet Stores Junction in August 1960 is Franco-Crosti '9F' 2-10-0 No. 92021, whose pre-heater has been blanked off, with a Chaddesden-Wellingborough freight. The sheet and tarpaulin factory from which the 'box took its name, together with a fan of four sidings, is behind the signalbox. The photographer is standing on the south curve and looking towards Derby.

J.A. Wade

prone to answering the wrong bell. When this happened, a quick wiggle of the block indicator would suffice. An illuminated track diagram was situated above the block shelf; some boxes of lesser importance had a non- illuminated diagram.

Sheet Stores Junction signal box, named after the nearby factory, which manufactured and repaired tarpaulins and sheeting to protect loaded open wagons, was also the only signalbox in the Trent district that had electricity. It was 8.7 miles from Derby and was on the east side in the middle of the junction where the Derby-Leicester line was bisected by trains crossing from the Trent direction onto the Castle Donington branch. There was a 60 m.p.h. limit for main-line trains, in contrast to the severe speed restriction of 15 m.p.h. to and from Trent and also onto and off the Castle Donington branch. The 36-lever frame signalbox, where a degree of regulating competence was required, was in such close proximity to the up line that at night it was almost impossible to obtain the engine numbers of fast up trains, despite the provision of a 150 watt bulb number-taking light. Indeed, many country located signal boxes had only gas lighting, others having to rely on paraffin for illumination whilst engine or local trip working was relied upon to deliver drinking water. A lighted handlamp was kept outside the door of the signal box during the hours of darkness, cleaned and trimmed daily by the control reporter. Broad wooden steps, with cast-iron treads marked 'Midland Railway', led up to the signalbox. Once inside, it became apparent that it was not large. There was a single stove, adequate for a box of this size, off-centre at the far end adjacent to where the control reporter was located. The interior was in stark contrast to the signal boxes at Trent North and Trent South, which were twice as long; both boxes had an additional fireplace, although this was seldom lit even in the harshest of winters. They did not compare as well as the brick-built centrally heated signal box with integral toilet and washing facilities enjoyed by the signalmen at Stapleford & Sandiacre, Toton Centre, Toton Junction and Toton East boxes.

There were different coloured levers in signal boxes, red for the home signal, red with a white band for the starter, yellow for the distant signal, black for points and blue for facing point locking. They were supplemented in every signal box by two or three (depending upon the size of the box) white levers, which were spares. I was initially told to operate one of the white levers at intervals to clear the smoke from the nearby Red Hill Tunnel. How gullible could one be?

All trains and light engines were reported to Nottingham Control, and trains and light engines to and from the Derby area were reported to Derby District Control. Neither control office had readily available the locomotive numbers of engines working Class 1,2 and 3 trains, unless they originated locally, when the power controller could supply the information to the section controller. Otherwise the Line Manager's Office (Divisional Control) at Derby would need to be approached for the relevant details. Certain section controllers were not particularly receptive to those requests. All was not lost though; after a few weeks I struck up a rapport with the box lad at Loughborough, Frank Cassell. He was in a similar position to myself as his signal box was extremely close to the down main line and he was unable to observe the engine numbers of fast trains, we would then exchange details as necessary although not all trains that passed his 'box came by Sheet Stores Junction.

Frank was pretty adept at arranging an itinerary, making certain that the requisite forms were completed and authorised, before purchasing privilege tickets at the respective booking office, supplementing the free travel pass. Some1,377 miles were covered on this foray to Stornoway on the Isle of Lewis in 1958.

Bed & Breakfast in Edinburgh for 14 shillings (70p). High Tea 6 shillings (30p).

Engine No.	Journey
DMU	Draycott & Breaston-Crewe
46206	Crewe-Perth 'The Royal Highlander' (46252 Euston-Crewe)
44704/44705	Perth-Inverness
54487/44719	Inverness-Kyle of Lochalsh
Loch Seaforth	Ferry-Kyle of Lochalsh-Stornoway-Mallaig
62011	Mallaig-Fort William
61789/44972	Fort William-Glasgow
60904	Glasgow-Edinburgh 'The North Briton' (60012 from Edinburgh)
61322	Edinburgh-North Queensferry
45640	North Queensferry-Edinburgh
60507	Edinburgh-Dundee
xxxxx	Dundee-Perth-Crewe
DMU	Crewe-Draycott & Breaston

A further sojourn, also making use of free and reduced rate facilities was to Antwerp. On that occasion Eric Nicholson – who I had come across when relieving him at Ilkeston South Junction – made all the necessary arrangements. I well remember we stayed overnight at the Bedford hotel in London before going across on the ferry the following morning.

I vividly remember turning on the radio in the hotel room at 9 p.m. to hear the continuity announcer Robin Boyle on the then BBC Light Programme proclaim, "And now, Your Hundred Best Tunes, introduced by Alan Keith". Alan introduced the programme for 44 years to which I was a regular listener until his death on 18th March 2003.

The last tenants of the station house at Sawley Crossing until its demolition in the late 1960s were the Baxter's'. It was where my grandfather lived during his tenure there as stationmaster. Gas lit, toilet at the bottom of the garden that was emptied on a regular basis by the local council with drinking water being extracted by means of an old fashioned pump in the kitchen. John Baxter, the youngest of four was at the time, and still is a close friend, indeed, on my visits to Long Eaton now, he still pops round for a chat with the usual piece of cake. We reminisce about those halcyon days in which I followed his hobby of saving King Edward V11 (1902-1910) pennies, those being easily distinguishable from that of King George as 'Ted's' head faced the opposite way, with 1904 being the least common date. Queen Victoria coins had two different designs as a matter of interest; the earlier and again the least common were those with her hair done in a bun. I still have some today. My hoard amounted to some four thousand Edward/Victoria pennies, almost £17 in today's value. When it came to cashing them in around about the late 1950s, I took them in a shopping bag on my bicycle to the Trustee Savings Bank in Long Eaton, only to be informed that they would not accept them unless tendered in five shilling copper bags, each one holding sixty pennies. As can be appreciated there was certainly some weight there and fortunately the sturdy leather shopping bag held on the journey home. Most of the pennies were subsequently disposed of at the local post office where mother had a newspaper delivery round. Later when telegraph and booking clerk at Trent I started collecting silver coins and amassed a considerable amount of silver pre-1920 coins tendered by the passengers booking tickets.

*   *   *

John Baxter was not a bad footballer; he had a trial with Coventry City and was in the forces with Johnny Byrne who played for Crystal Palace. For most of his national service John was stationed at Kineton in Warwickshire and came home most weekends. I then had the onerous task on those Sunday nights around eleven o'clock, of transporting him on my crossbar from the station house to Risley a couple of miles away where he would pick up his lift back to camp. Not an easy trek when carrying a suitcase and on a rising gradient into the bargain. Strangely enough, on the theme of two on a bike, back in 1957 when, for whatever reason with the roles reversed, I was being carried on the crossbar of

BR Standard Class 7P No. 70021 *'Morning Star'* hurries through the closed Sawley station with a St. Pancras-Manchester Central express in July 1958 shortly after six 'Britannia' Pacifics had replaced the 'Royal Scots' on the Midland Division and were allocated to Trafford Park (9E).
J.A. Wade

his bicycle when a policeman halted our progress, needless to say a summons ensued. The outcome of the subsequent court hearing – we both pleaded guilty by letter and were fined ten shillings (50p) each – was reported in the Long Eaton Advertiser, the opening sentence read; "We shall get there quicker was the explanation given by John Baxter when stopped by P.C ... "

We both had further brushes with the penal code a year or two later, John for riding his cycle without lights and I was apprehended, this time for carrying Geoff Wall an ex-control reporter at Toton Centre on my crossbar, resulting in a £1 fine.

A further reshuffle of express motive power took place in July 1958 when six 'Britannia' Pacifics were procured, Nos. 70004 'William Shakespeare' and 70014 'Iron Duke' from Stewarts Lane, 70015 'Apollo', 70017 'Arrow', and 70021 'Morning Star' from Cardiff (Canton) and 70042 'Lord Roberts' from Stratford; and transferred to the Midland Division and allocated to Trafford Park (9E), Nos. 70004, 70014, 70017 and 70042 initially having been stopped off at Kentish Town for a couple of weeks. This enabled the 'Royal Scots' to be returned from Kentish Town back to the Western Division. Three further 'Britannias', Nos. 70031 'Byron', 70032 'Tennyson' and 70033 ' Charles Dickens', appeared later, bringing the stud at Trafford Park to nine.

* * *

Diesel locomotives were also appearing in ever increasing numbers and not only from BR Workshops. The Metropolitan-Vickers Type 2 Co-Bo 1,200hp units with a top speed of 75 m.p.h. had a relatively short spell, operating in pairs on the St. Pancras-Manchester expresses and also Britain's fastest freight, the 'Condor', which began its career on 16th March 1959. Running between Hendon and Gushetfaulds on Mondays to Fridays passing through Trent at 9.50 p.m. on the down journey and 2.45 a.m. in reverse direction on Sundays to Thursdays, the train initially conveyed 27 roller bearing fitted, vacuum braked 'Platefit' wagons loaded with containers, although the loading was reduced later. At first, specific instructions regarding the traction for the 'Condor' was, that if one of the diesels failed before the start of the journey, then two Class '5' 4-6-0s must be substituted for both diesels, but if a diesel failed en-route, it could be replaced by a single Class '5', which had to be coupled behind the surviving diesel.

The first BR/Sulzer Type 4 'Peak' Class 2,300hp diesel-electric 1Co-Co1 locomotive was outshopped from Derby in the Summer of 1959 and after a naming ceremony at

A St. Pancras-Manchester Central express passing Draycott in June 1959 with twin Metropolitan-Vickers 1,200hp Co-Bo units.
J.A. Wade

Metropolitan-Vickers twin diesels on the viaduct over the River Trent with a Manchester-St. Pancras express *circa 1960*. In the distance a freight train is just visible on the up goods line.

J.A. Wade

Carlisle, D1 Scafell Pike returned to base for trials on the Derby-Manchester route. Together with the other nine members of the Class they worked up the Midland Main Line to St. Pancras before being released to the Western Lines of the LMR. D2 had been experimentally uprated to 2,500hp and all the Class received names appertaining to mountains in England and Wales.

Having done my initial training at Sheet Stores Junction a year earlier, interspersed with duties at other locations, I had a self-belief in the competence required. Working both the block equipment and the frame, there was an element of trust between man and 'boy'. I was allocated the shift with Doug (of the mounties) Lawson; his regular lad with whom he had been reliant upon, to a certain extent had left for pastures new, so there was a transitional period to negotiate. Doug was a nervous chain-smoker approaching retirement age; he was a fan of the singer David Whitfield and a follower of Sheffield Wednesday Football Club. As the months unfolded, my impetuosity got the better of me and our relationship degenerated. A switch to another shift became necessary; we no longer saw eye to eye on various issues, primarily, the regulation of trains, which, in fairness to Doug, was not, and should not have been any concern of mine, although I could not ignore it. Nonetheless, if matters did not go my way, I would turn sulky, which was no fun for me, and less so for the signalman.

The volume of telephone reports transmitted and received warranted the employment of a signal box lad (officially a junior control reporter) who, at Sheet Stores Junction would compile a the train recorder's book while at Trent Station South 'box the Train Register Book would also be his responsibility. In addition to disseminating train reports to other signal boxes and the Control Offices at Derby and Nottingham, there were daily chores to be undertaken, cleaning and servicing the hand lamp, dusting the lever frame and shelf housing the block bells and instruments, polishing the brasses, cleaning the fire, replenishing the coal scuttle and sweeping up. Whereas the floor and windows would be done in-house at Sheet Stores the station porters would undertake those duties at Trent Station South and North Junction signal boxes.

* * *

Reports of express trains passing Chesterfield, Millers Dale, Melton Mowbray and leaving Leicester, were received at Sheet Stores from the telegraph office at Trent. These were recorded and passed on to the signalman, as were details of all trains departing from Derby station, which were put out on an omnibus telephone circuit using a series of short rings by the control reporter at Derby 'A' box. My duties then included advising the signalmen at Trent Junction and Ratcliffe Junction signal boxes of class 1 & 3 trains leaving Derby and also of any other trains going their way when they passed Spondon Junction. The signalman at the latter 'box reported all trains to Sheet Stores, who, after advising the signalman, would then inform the control office at Nottingham. Having rest days, which did not coincide gave both parties a break from each other's company. Indeed, it was always an interesting experience to work with some relief signalmen who only came to Sheet Stores on very infrequent occasions and often sought my support, which I readily gave. Alf Long was now my mate, a quiet individual of few words, forever reading and studying form of racehorses. He seemed to have a phobia about answering the telephone, so much so that if I was washing the floor or for whatever reason was outside the signal box, the phone continued to ring until I got to it. Alf later transferred to North Erewash Junction where he would be alone; he was more at home with that arrangement. John Turley from Trent Junction took his place.

* * *

The other regular signalman at Sheet Stores was Alf (Taffy) Jones, known as the Welsh wizard; he rolled his own cigarettes, had his breeches backside hanging out, shoelaces undone and was constantly jabbering in some 'foreign' language. For all that, he had a heart of gold and the father and son relationship with his control reporter endeared him to many. His mate, Ernie Phillips, an elderly and often sick man, would battle to work when others would have stayed at home, frequently having to stop two or three times for a blow up on the ¼ mile walk from his home at Sawley. This was in stark contrast to the couple of moaning minnies at the next 'box, Trent South, where strangely enough, Alf would go on promotion a few years later. What a small world this is. On the overnight Nottingham to Newquay train in 1971, and peering out of the carriage window at around 5.45 a.m. when passing St. Blazey; who would be gazing out of the signal box but Alf Jones; greetings being hurriedly exchanged.

I now had green card men either side; much to his displeasure, Doug Lawson had inherited one, supposedly a patentee and a storyteller into the bargain.

I welcomed the opportunity of working with a variety of signalmen; some excellent, others less so and a few were very indifferent. This inference being to their regulating capability, some locations demanding a higher level than others, with Sheet Stores Junction a prime example. I well remember Bill Beers coming to Sheet Stores on promotion. An avid Shirley Bassey fan, his regulating knowledge was limited in the extreme, being ensconced at Toton East Junction, seldom if ever signalling a passenger train, where the only regulation involved a freight train departing from the East yard and a Beyer-Garratt clanking up the (other) Lickey. There was certainly a learning curve here and Bill did find it hard going coming to terms with the main line.

A source of fun in those early BR days was the annual Toton and District Staff Outing. Usually two trains ran from outstations to a seaside resort until support waned in the early 1960s. It was normally a case of 'break out the booze' when the trains were barely out of the Toton/Trent area. And this before 8 o'clock! At the time this free travel was over and above the annual allocation, which then only allowed one 'foreign' free ticket over another region's metals. A further example of this was in 1957, the resultant boundary changes saw the Sheffield and Leeds districts come under the auspices of the North Eastern Region; this then constituted a 'foreign' pass, however, travel to Carlisle via this route was permitted.

At this time Holiday Expresses were still evident and operated from principal stations during the school holiday periods. These special trains complete with headboard – 'City of Nottingham', etc – left each morning to selected places of interest and popular seaside resorts. Each train conveyed a Cafeteria car and was hauled by a spruced up locomotive. A comprehensive ticket was issued for the complete weekly programme, although I don't recollect knowing anyone who used the service, which, judging by the number of coaches and faces at the window, loaded pretty well. Starlight Specials', cheap excursion trains ran from London to Glasgow and Edinburgh; the overnight services which were first introduced in 1953 ran during the summer months were routed over both the Midland and Great Central lines and were well patronised.

* * *

'Bunking' Motive Power Depots was the norm for hundreds of train spotters each weekend, Crewe North and South sheds being a Mecca. I remember writing in 1957 to the District Commercial Manager (DCM) at Derby and again three years later requesting permission to visit Crewe Motive Power Depots. The reply to each cited – technical difficulties in connection with works taking place at Crewe – as the reason for the refusal, although parties affiliated to various Clubs might well have enjoyed access. A further request to the DCM in 1961, whilst still implying the no visit scenario to Crewe Depots, requested that applications be submitted through my local staff office. The shed foreman at Crewe North (5A), and Crewe South (5B), no doubt had their own method to superintend the unauthorised weekend incursions, tantamount to a game of cat and mouse.

Many would get through completely unscathed; others would adopt a more refined approach by enquiring permission from the shed foreman. There were many of course, who, for whatever reason waited outside the gates eager to hear from those purporting to have been round, details of their adventurism. Permits could be obtained to visit Crewe Locomotive Works on Sundays at a fee of sixpence (2½p), the proceeds of which went to the Crewe Railway Charity Fund.

A vital piece of equipment, necessary when visiting locomotive installations for the first time was The British Locomotive Shed Directory, a definitive guide with directions from the nearest station compiled by a Flight Lieutenant. With its comprehensive street guide, bus numbers and distance including walking time it was an essential part in producing an itinerary for depot visits. Wearing uniform was also contemplated when visiting motive power depots without the necessary authority, simulating erroneously a purpose for being there. The nearest I came to that was to wear my fawn mackintosh on a visit to Crewe. On the theme of uniform, whilst being mandatory for many including station staff, a few of the signalmen I came across thought fit to wear their own apparel,

THE BRITISH LOCOMOTIVE SHED DIRECTORY

A COMPLETE GUIDE TO ALL MAIN LINE LOCOMOTIVE SHEDS & WORKS IN GT. BRITAIN

NINTH EDITION PRICE 6/-

likening the uniform material to sackcloth. On the initial measurement form the term vest appeared, I wrongly likened this to the garment worn under the shirt and appended the length accordingly. Fortunately, the sleeved waistcoat fitted a treat although the measurement quoted probably raised an eyebrow or two at the factory.

* * *

But to return to Sheet Stores – Owing to the short block sections involved – 933 yards to Sawley Junction and 811 yards to Trent Junction – special arrangements were applicable to working the down road between those signal boxes. In the 'box at Sheet Stores there was a brass disc, with an inscription on the face, which, by changing position, gave an indication that the signalman at Sawley Junction had cleared his distant signal. This was the necessary authority for Sheet Stores then to clear his distant signal. To amplify this, a couple of jar/bottle tops were affixed to the disc; these would clank together when the signal was operated giving an audible sound to the signalman. This did not prevent the distant signal worked from Sheet Stores being cleared before this occurred, but the local instructions stated this must not be done. One of the signalman at Sawley Junction, Jack Stevens, only had only one arm, but my goodness he didn't half make those screw tops dance when pulling his distant signal off.

There was a slightly different arrangement at Trent Junction; at this signal box the signalman was physically prevented from pulling off his distant signal, as it was under-bolted or slotted by the release from Sheet Stores. Perhaps, for the benefit of some readers, I should explain what this means. Let us take three signal boxes, A.B.C. In the example, 'A' is Sawley Junction, 'B' is Sheet Stores Junction and 'C' is Trent Junction. When the signalman at A pulled off his distant signal, a brass disc dropped from the vertical to horizontal position in box 'B'. The disc was only a few inches in size and was not however at eye level – hence the screw tops. The object was to attract the signalman's attention. Although this arrangement did not physically prevent the signalman at 'box 'B' from releasing his distant signal, working instructions at 'B' stipulated that he must not.

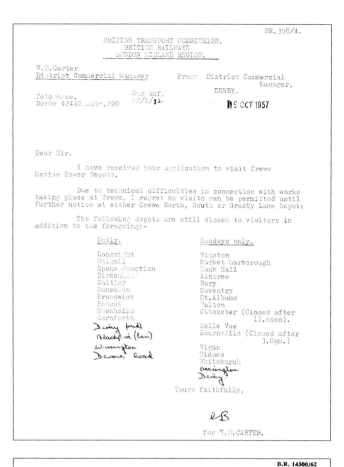

The signalman at 'C' was prevented from pulling off his distant until it was released from 'B'. This was done by a (underbolting/slotting) mechanism in the signal box that indicated the position, on or off, of B's distant signal. The object of the Absolute Block signalling system is to prevent more than one train being in a block section on the same line at the same time. Prior to the despatch of a train from 'box 'A', the signalman there, provided that he has received the 'Train out of section' signal for the previous train and the block indicator is in the normal position, must call the attention of 'box 'B' and, having obtained it, send the proper 'Is line clear' signal. If the line is clear at 'B', the signalman there may acknowledge the signal and place the block indicator to the 'Line clear' position. Until the signalman gave 'Line clear', the signalman at the 'box in rear would be unable to release his signal controlling the entrance to the section. This 'safeguard' did not apply at Sheet Stores with movements onto and off the Castle Donington branch as signals could be cleared without the requisite 'Line clear' position on the block indicator. I recall accepting a train from Lock Lane Crossing, pegging the block indicator to 'Train on Line' and the signalman there was able to release his starting signal. That to my mind was not conducive to safe working. When the signalman at Sheet Stores received the 'Train entering section' bell signal from Trent Junction or Trent Station South Junction, he would send Sawley Junction a special bell signal, 1-2-1, denoting 'Train approaching', which was immediately sent on to Sawley Crossing Signal Box. The signalman at Sawley Crossing, who had previously 'arrested' the 'Is line clear' bell signal, would then send it on to Draycott, the next 'box. He would then close the level crossing gates and pull off his signals when the train had been accepted. By the time this had taken place, an express would be approaching the signal box at Sawley Junction with the driver within sight of the distant colour light signal situated beyond the station platform and operated by Sawley Crossing.

* * *

Recording engine numbers at Sheet Stores Signal Box and getting paid for doing so couldn't be bad. Actually working there was a thrill. I could and did work the box as good as the next and better than most, and, as mentioned earlier, tended to be rather put out if a move was blocked when clearly I thought it should have taken place. There was no requirement however to record the engine numbers of express, ordinary passenger and parcels trains. I, however, wanted the lot, including the originating and destination of all freight trains, it being sufficient just to log the engine number, route and the time. With Toton marshalling yard a couple of miles away, one of the biggest flows of traffic through Trent station and over Sheet Stores Junction consisted of coal trains to the CEGB power stations at Castle Donington, Repton & Willington and Drakelow, also traffic for Washwood Heath and the Western Region via the exchange at Bordesley Junction. They had to be staged between the interval Nottingham to Leicester and Derby passenger services and the London-Manchester expresses. These heavy freight trains were best kept on the move; however, the signalman's biggest handicap was that he had no precise indication of the train's whereabouts at the time it was offered. As far as regulating was concerned, Norman Earl, a rest-day relief signalman, had the right philosophy, "Give 'em a run!"

It could be coming from a stand at Trent North or be dragging its way out of Toton yard with the two level crossings to negotiate. The signalman therefore had to decide fairly quickly when offered a train whether he was going to run it or not, with due cognisance if an express was imminent. Often the signalman at Trent North would use the telephone to ascertain if a path was available for the freight train. The gradient from Trent South to Sheet Stores, rising at 1-in-586, not particularly steep, changing to 1-in-220; this was sufficient to cause difficulty if an engine started slipping. The 15 m.p.h. speed

Red Hill tunnel and Trent Junction signalbox provide the backdrop as LMS Class 8F 2-8-0 No. 48698 approaches Sheet Stores Junction signalbox with a Toton-Washwood Heath freight, circa 1959.

The gradient from Trent South to Sheet Stores rising at 1-in-586 changing to 1-in-220, although not particularly steep was sufficient to cause difficulty if an engine started slipping. An unidentified Stanier 6P5F 2-6-0 approaches the signalbox with a train of pipes from Stanton Ironworks to Washwood Heath.

(Left) New signalbox nearing completion at Lock Lane Crossing on the existing site that necessitated a temporary box (where a cycle is propped up against) housing the block instruments. When the new structure was commissioned the crossing gates still had to be opened and closed manually. November 1957.
J.A. Wade

(Right) The signalbox at Lock Lane Crossing was less than two years old when this photograph was taken as ex-L.N.W. Class 7F 0-8-0 No. 49444 rumbles by with a Beeston-Washwood Heath mineral train on 12th March 1959.
Tony Smith

restriction through Trent station and the more severe 10 m.p.h. over Trent Station South Junction would always be a hindrance to the progress of a heavy coal train. In the early morning watching the 5.50 a.m. Toton-Wichnor, 6.7 a.m. Toton-Branston and the 6.20 a.m. Toton-Foleshill, one or other coming from a stand at Trent North giving their all, fighting for adhesion on the rise to Sheet Stores during times of poor rail conditions, was a sight and sound to behold. Invariably with safety valves lifting, the fireman in his seat, he had done his bit for a while, the engine would then be shouting its way towards Lock Lane Crossing, a cheery wave from the guard after refilling his pipe and we were ready for the next one.

Depending on the distance between signal boxes, it was usual to offer a train to the next 'box when received from the 'box in rear, or when receiving 'Train Entering Section' bell signal from that 'box. Circumstances were different between Lock Lane Crossing and Sheet Stores. Although Lock Lane had received 'Train Entering Section' from Castle Donington, some 250 yards short of three miles away, he would not offer the train to Sheet Stores until it came into view. Assuming that Sheet Stores had accepted it, the signalman at Lock Lane would then 'dash' down the 'box steps and manually close the crossing gates to road traffic. So far so good, invariably though, the impetus would be lost, by the time 'Bombardier' Billy Wells had passed the time of day with Mrs so-and-so or the vicar and was back in the signal box the train had passed his distant signal. This of course could prove crucial, and the delay associated with the driver of the freight train sighting the distant signal at caution often did have implications at the Sheet Stores end if a passenger train was due. One way around this problem during daylight hours was to look out for the smoke and steam of an approaching train, which, owing to the curva-

ture of the line, could be seen in the distance from Sheet Stores. Then, to encourage the signalman at Lock Lane that the train would be accepted – in other words close the gates and pull off. The level crossing was not particularly busy with road traffic except at the weekends when Trent Lock proved a popular haunt for weekend recreation and leisure pursuits.

By and large, many freight trains would come from a stand at Lock Lane owing to the circumstances prevailing at Sheet Stores, namely the importance and frequency of the interval service of passenger trains from Derby to Nottingham and Lincoln, and the St. Pancras to Manchester expresses. Short freight trains would be allowed to run up to the starting signal whilst others were kept back at the home signal. When obtaining suitable paths was relatively tight, it was usual to ask the Lock Lane signalman to 'start it up', the train would then be on the move when accepted and so reduce the time taken to reach Sheet Stores.

A driver renowned for crawling about the system was George Pearson, who was in the 'old man's link' at Toton and worked local trips to Chaddesden, Nottingham, etc. On many occasions, when he was driving a Toton-Chaddesden freight train, with a clear road from as far back as Long Eaton station, he would finally put in an appearance after what seemed an eternity since his train was first described. Ambling along with no sense of urgency, safety valves blowing off for all they were worth and the fireman looking totally fed up with proceedings. We would stand at the window glowering at the driver and endeavouring to urge him on as there was on occasions a passenger train not far behind. Pearson appeared totally oblivious to the gesticulations; no doubt the District Motive Power Superintendent interviewed him on more than one occasion over his habitual slow running, which would inevitably result in delay to other trains. I could never understand the statement 'bare margin'. The time allowance required for a freight train to precede an express from Sheet Stores to Spondon Junction was nineteen minutes. Either the freight had the requisite margin or it hadn't.

The Control Office, despite its name, was not directly concerned with detailed regulation, although, being dependent on ground reports, the Control only had a general overview. The on-the-ground regulation was in the hands of the signalmen, which was clearly the right approach. Perceived by many railwaymen as faceless individuals, those in the Control Office were only able to disseminate information, which had been fed into the Control by whatever means and from information gathered internally. Often the Section Controller would instruct Sheet Stores not to let any more freight trains off the Castle Donington branch owing to the reception roads and goods lines to Beeston or Toton yards being full. Some trains would then stand on the branch end for long periods and on occasions a relief train crew had to be sent to relieve the train. There was a trainmen's relief cabin at the west end of Trent station and Control were very well aware that many signalmen would not allow train crews to wait in the signal box, other than to carry out Rule 55. This was perfectly understandable, judging by the conditions some relief cabins were left in. However, a polite request to the signalman by enginemen, with minimal waiting time for the train they were to relieve, was often agreed to.

*   *   *

The tarpaulin factory at Sheet Stores was serviced daily by a 'trip' from Chaddesden which also shunted the coal/scrap yards en route. The trip arrived late in the afternoon and would be stationary down the 'hole' for ages, and usually appeared at a most inopportune time to start shunting. This work involved occupation of the up line, which

Midland Class 3F 0-6-0 No.
43735 traversing the north-
curve in evening sunshine with
6.45 p.m. Sheet Stores-Chad-
desden pick-up freight on 14th
July 1959.
Tony Smith

impacted on trains from the Derby direction and also off the Castle Donington branch. During foggy weather this became increasingly difficult; although the main line was track circuited, the points, just inside the sidings, were not. There was an illuminated track diagram at Sheet Stores Junction, which was activated by movements on the running lines, but during foggy weather the trip engine could be standing foul of the main line if it was standing on the points that connected the sidings to the main line. Because there was no telephone available, it was a case of walking down to ascertain that the movement was inside clear.

A.W. (Tony) Smith, the stationmaster at Trent, affectionately known as 'Ethel' seemed to have a fixation regarding the trip and put in quite a lot of time trying to chivvy up proceedings, without a great deal of success. Thinking back, perhaps it had something to do with the time staff finished work at the factory before shunting could commence. With buildings either side of the main line, a small-gauge track with hand-pushed trucks was used to ferry the cargo under the main line between buildings. With the canal nearby, a lagoon was used in the yard as a means of testing the waterproofing of the tarpaulins and sheeting. Rumour had it that during a period of heavy snow Alf Long actually rode into the pond. He was never forthcoming when questioned about this.

One night, when Tony Smith was on one of his nocturnal jaunts, we were caught napping. My sister Jane had loaned me her Pye radio that was battery and mains operated. The two batteries were quite expensive and didn't last all that long, however, this was academic at Sheet Stores where electricity was available. Shortly after ten o'clock that night, the stationmaster was at the top of the steps before we realised it, the jungle telegraph hadn't picked this one up. On entering the 'box, he said "hello" or similar, and then promptly asked about the radio which was playing away on the shelf at the far end of the signal box where I performed my control reporting duties. He then proceeded to tell us that the use of radios was not allowed and contravened the rules, of which we should have been well aware. This I acknowledged and promptly closed the top of the radio, which silenced it. Because it was quite dark at that end of the 'box, I was certain Tony did not realise that it was working off the mains electric supply. One tale that did the rounds, concerned the footpath from North Erewash Junction to Trent station, a distance of some 600 yards. Gas lit at varying intervals and deemed no cycling, one night Slim Everly, a 'box lad at Trent South, was negotiating this route when he collided with a cyclist riding in the opposite direction. After they had dusted themselves down, Slim was surprised to see that the other cyclist was none other than Tony Smith; needless to say, few words of comfort were exchanged.

Shift patterns varied from 'box to 'box. Sawley Junction, Trent South and Trent Junction worked a clockwise shift; this meant that the signalman at Sheet Stores worked to a different colleague every three weeks; Trent North also worked anticlockwise. With the Control office working the same shift pattern, a rapport developed with Albert Jones in the Derby District Office and Freddie Pratt at Nottingham. Both were followers of Derby County Football Club and we agreed to meet one Saturday at the bus stop outside Derby station to go to the football match. The advice I was given was to look out for a couple of six foot three individuals. Sure enough, there were not too many men that met this description so I approached a couple of likely looking gents and my guess was correct. I wasn't sure just what to say, and after the briefest of introductions I remember saying to Fred, "What about this Toton standing on the branch?" Not the most appropriate remark to have made! Fortunately, the arrival of the Upperdale Road trolley bus ended the conversation. I realised from this encounter that these faceless individuals were actually human; seven years later I would link up with them in what would be a highlight of almost forty years on the railway.

In those days Derby County Football Club frequently travelled by rail to away fixtures, particularly to the capital, and I used to combine a day in London with visits to the termini at King's Cross, Euston and Liverpool Street, before going to the match. I seem to recall that the 'Rams' never fared very well in the metropolis.

The grandeur of St. Pancras station was a joy to behold; in many ways perhaps the grandest of London's termini. Opened on 1st October 1868, it stands as a spectacular memorial to the days of the Midland railway. Enhanced by the Victorian Gothic Midland Grand Hotel designed by Sir George Gilbert Scott and opened on 5th May 1873, the magnificent giant single span train shed roof was constructed by the Butterley Company in Derbyshire, some 240 feet wide, 689 feet long with an apex height of 100 feet, engineer William Henry Barlow could justifiably feel proud of this architectural construction – a railway cathedral. The mellifluous tones of the station announcer was as if he was addressing every passenger personally, his voice reverberating around the giant roof span adding to the splendour of just being present, with sights and sounds to savour. Even the 'Jubilee' on the 6.30 p.m. departure to Derby seemed to respect the occasion by keeping its steam under control, the tank engine at the buffer stop end of the platform also performing likewise as the footballers settled down in the Restaurant Car in readiness for their evening meal as we travelled home.

During the summer of 1947, on the approaches to St. Pancras 240 yards of track were completely relayed over a period of fourteen Sundays from June to September. This involved 40 sets of points and 50 crossings, all the trackwork being manufactured by Taylor Bros of Sandiacre (adjacent to the Up yard at Toton) as a built up and timbered layout, the material being prefabricated in sidings situated near to the junction at St. Pancras.

* * *

There was a four-man permanent-way gang at Sheet Stores, oiling points, controlled burning of vegetation, the daily walk along the length to replace any missing keys, and other work including lifting the track and meticulously measuring out chippings into a tin before shovelling them underneath the wooden sleepers. On what was also referred to as jointed track, there was the annual removal of fishplates to enable the bolts to be greased to assist movement when expansion took take place. During heavy frost and snow, the permanent-way men would also keep the braziers stoked up at water columns, although some columns were the responsibility of the Locomotive or Traffic Departments. Other work included the clearance of snow from points, general snow clearance and salting foot crossings. Most of the gang were getting on in years; Arthur Higginbottom could never understand why his pocket watch did not show the same time as the clock in the signal box. "Hey-up Jack! C'mon its dinnertime", and often they would go for snap an hour early much to the consternation of the ganger. The platelayers over the system as a whole were extremely dedicated, having great pride in their 'lengths', mani-festing and punctiliously hand-tending the ballast to provide a safe cess. The only obstacle to be encountered would be a lump of coal that had fallen off the locomotives. This good housekeeping was appreciated by those who chose to cycle or walk in the cess, to get to their place of work. Prizes were awarded for the best-kept length in the district.

It was whilst at Sheet Stores that I first came across Raymond Bennett, who was working on the permanent way section between Sawley Junction and Sawley Crossing, he was also the nominated fog signalman for the up outer distant controlled from Sheet Stores. This signal was located at the west end of the station platform at Sawley Junc-tion. As this distant signal could not be worked for trains going towards Trent, it was an extremely busy fogging post. Most signal boxes had a fog marking point, where this was obscured or, where not specified, the signalman could not see for a distance of 200 yards, the fog signalman had to be sent for. When a distant signal was at caution, or a stop signal at danger the fog signalman had to have a detonator on the line and exhibit a hand signal of the appropriate colour. When the signal was placed to all clear he removed the deto-nator and exhibited a green hand signal to the driver.

Fog in those days was, 'a three-way killer with no holds barred. It chokes you. It chills you. It blinds you'. The old-fashioned yellow pea-souper fogs whose density did not lift for days on end were potent in the extreme for the elderly and those with breathing diffi-culties. Effacing all sounds, when an approaching train could barely be discerned until it arrived in the platform. Visibility did vary, however, it was generally acknowledged that when the Barton buses, a bus undertaking that operated between Derby and Nottingham and throughout the Nottingham area, were called in off the road and ceased to run, conditions were very bad, with some firms sending their workers home early. Some fog signalmen like Ray would report on their own volition without waiting to be called, while others would bide their time until advised by the caller-up who was contacted through the Telegraph Office at Trent. In later years it became a standing joke that Raymond would report when it was misty and leave his post when sunny. Ray (Bunny) was a Breaston lad like myself; he had broken his service with the railway, having had a spell with Roberts scrap merchants, whose businesses was at Sawley Crossing and adjacent to the coal yard at Draycott & Breaston station. He would be working alongside his brother-in-law Lewis White and there was no love lost between them then, and neither was there in later years.

My first encounter with Lew was in the Sawley Arms public house in 1958, there was Ku-Can card school(s) on Friday/Saturday/Sunday evenings and at lunchtimes on Saturday and Sundays. Ku-Can is a game played for money that was not on the permitted list. Roughly every three weeks I would make the trip to Sawley from Plymouth for a convivial evening at the card table at the Railway Inn, the Sawley Arms long since closed. Accompanied by his faithful dog Barney, Lew, widowed for many years, and with the loss of sight in one eye, still took his place in the card school until in his early nineties, we being the only two left from the original members. Lewis had of course mellowed over the years, from being a cantankerous and argumentative cuss, a primary cause of the fric-tion at the scrap yards, to a man with remarkable powers at remembering not only which cards had been played, but who had picked them up, quite phenomenal. Lewis passed away in 2005, the end of an era. During times of severe frost, Ray reminded me that there used to be a list of volunteers required to travel to Loughborough to keep the water troughs from freezing over. Never one to miss an opportunity to earn an extra bob or two, he offered his services.

I once asked him what implements were used in carrying out these duties. "Anything you could get hold of", he replied and went on to explain that it wasn't unusual for the gang to walk up and down inside the troughs to keep them free from ice. Crampons were supplied to assist movements in what at times were treacherous underfoot conditions. Some years later and until he retired in July 1993, Ray was an operator on a tamping and lining machine. We have been friends since our first meeting in those early days at Sheet Stores; his interest in football however, we both went to watch Derby County on a regular basis years earlier, has since waned.

The most notable feature on the late turn at Sheet Stores, certainly the highlight of the week as far as I was concerned, was the running of the afternoon Class 'H' freight train from Wellingborough to Chaddesden. Worked by a Derby train crew, who had travelled up in the 10.25 a.m. ex Manchester Central, the train invariably ran before time. It was usually standing at Ratcliffe Junction on the down goods line waiting to come out behind 141 express 4.25 p.m. St. Pancras-Manchester Central. The 12 week link cycle over a three week period produced four different sets of enginemen, three of which could he guaranteed to run like the wind with the fourth not far behind. We came to know which crew to expect and soon built up a healthy supply of hand-cloths, these were thrown from the engine as the freight stormed past, an indication of the body language of the footplate men intimating that relief was required on arrival, the request being passed on to the Derby District Control. Greetings were exchanged at Ratcliffe Junction between 141 express hauled by a 'Britannia' (later it would be a Metro-Vick diesel) and the freight train with its usual Stanier 8F 2-8-0 hauling anything up to sixty wagons in length. Usually the freight would be emerging from Red Hill tunnel by the time 141 had cleared Sawley Crossing, just in time to see Sheet Stores clear the distant signal. In addition, a freight train would have been offered from Trent South for the Castle Donington branch, which would have been accepted at caution, likewise one from Lock Lane as well. There would also be a Beeston-Chaddesden freight in the wings in addition to the Sheet Stores trip trundling its way round the North Curve to Sawley Junction, with no path available until after the passage of 147, the 5.5 p.m. St. Pancras-Bradford Forster Square. We were conscious, of course, that the Beeston-Chaddesden was booked in front of the freight from Wellingborough, but as a branch train had been offered from Trent South, the Beeston-Chaddesden would have been on the goods line out of the way. Indeed, the trip was also timed to precede the freight from Wellingborough.

I have previously mentioned that detailed train regulation rests with the signalman and not the Control Office, and although the signalman at Sawley Junction had only one train to regulate, he would contact the Control as to when he could run the Sheet Stores trip off the North Curve. He obviously didn't want an ear bashing from the train crew for being detained there. On one occasion the freight from Wellingborough, running even earlier than usual found its way down the goods line from Trent Junction to Sheet Stores to wait for a path. 141 express (4.25 p.m. St. Pancras-Manchester) was three or four minutes late going by and by the time the freight had dragged its way out of the down goods line 147 (5.5 p.m. St. Pancras-Bradford) had already left Leicester, non-stop to Derby.

The freight then stopped outside the 'box, and the driver, who we knew as Sid (Stan was his mate), requested relief on arrival and would I inform the Control? The signalman – a relief man – was now beside himself having palpitations, "Tell him to get cracking" he cried and then came to the window and gesticulated to the driver to get a move on. "I'll not stop the express", shouted Sid, and with that up went the regulator and with

This picture, taken at Sheet Stores Junction in July 1958, shows a St. Pancras-Bradford Forster Square express with 'Jubilee' Class 6P 4-6-0 No. 45597 'Barbados', piloted by Stanier Class Class 5 4-6-0 No. 45101.
J.A. Wade

more than a full head of steam, the freight blasted its way towards Sawley Junction. The points were then reversed and a Toton-Washwood Heath coal train went onto the branch, whilst a train of empties for Beeston came from Lock Lane. 147 was getting ever closer, if it was to sight adverse signals then Draycott would be the place while the freight cleared Borrowash almost two and a half miles distance. The express was signalled at 7.4 p.m., signals were cleared and 147 emerged from Red Hill tunnel – double headed – just our luck. I rang the signalman at Borrowash for a progress report on the Wellingborough-Chaddesden; it had not reached there as yet. 147 passed Sheet Stores at 7.9 p.m. half a minute early, hauled by a Stanier 'Black 5' and a 'Jubilee'. After advising Derby 'A' box of the express, I tried Borrowash again a couple of minutes later, by which time 147 would be approaching Sawley Crossing within sight of the outer distant signal controlled from Draycott 'box. "Just passed, going like a bomb with the guard hanging on for grim death", said the signalman. It was a close-run thing the margin for a freight to precede an express from Sheet Stores to Spondon Junction was 19 minutes; on that occasion it was a good deal less than that. The Draycott-Borrowash block section was always a problem during fog when there was no fog signalman on duty at the down outer distant signal worked from Draycott 'box. This situation severely restricted the number of trains over the down line, thus effectively reducing line occupation. Although the previous train had passed Draycott, and the 'Train out of section' bell signal had been sent, the signalman there could not accept another train from Sawley Crossing, until he had received the 'Train out of Section signal' from Borrowash 2½ miles away; this was termed double-block working.

Motive power was ever changing: During 1959, Kentish Town (14B) received another batch of 'Royal Scots' as did Millhouses (19B), and Nottingham (16A) received its first allocation of Class '7P' locomotives. Towards the end of 1960 the 'Britannia' Pacifics were transferred back to the Western Lines; apparently they had not taken too kindly to regular service over the curves of the Derby-Manchester route. It would not be long before BR/Sulzer Type '4' diesels took charge of the expresses to and from St. Pancras.

* * *

On the B6005 Nottingham to Derby road there were two bridges over the railway at Draycott that were narrow and difficult to negotiate. Indeed, the one at the west end of the village was also set at an obtuse angle, both were demolished in the late 1950s, and whilst the work was being undertaken it necessitated all rail traffic being diverted over the

Civil engineering works in progress to replace the over-bridge at Draycott in May 1959 as Metropolitan Vickers Co-Bo 1,200 h.p. units D5701 & D5716 pass the site with a St. Pancras-Manchester Central express.
J.A. Wade

Castle Donington branch. The bridge at Draycott & Breaston station also meant extra work for the signalman at Sawley Crossing winding the gates, as he had to contend with additional road traffic for many weeks including the Barton bus service running between Derby and Nottingham.

Although the Castle
Donington line did not have a
regular passenger train service,
it was used for diversions,
owing to flooding on the line
at Draycott, or during
engineering operations. Here, a
Cravens two-car unit working
a Nottingham-Derby local on
25th September 1959.
J.A. Wade

The cleaning and trimming of signal lamps was an art in itself; unless done properly, the glass would soot up and so give off a poor light. John Hitchcock was the Trent area lamp man and drivers working through the district no doubt appreciated the time and effort which 'Johnny the Lamp' put into his work. Indicative of this, seldom was there a signal lamp out even in the harshest of conditions. Lamping was not a job for the faint-hearted, certainly vertigo was not an attribute, some signal posts rocked alarmingly when the signal was operated at the time the lamp man was near to the top of it.

The task had to undertaken whatever the weather, torrential rain, driving snow, gale force winds, fog and frost or a combination of any of them. Wet weather gear in those days was heavy and cumbersome, a far cry from today's lightweight apparel. Reeking of paraffin and with his cheeky grin Johnny was often asked as the heavens opened, "Which lighthouse are you relieving at today?"

*   *   *

The 'KGB' was not only to be found behind the Iron Curtain, it was also in evidence around the Trent district in the form of relief signalman Kenneth G. Bradford. Having worked with a variety of 'bobbies' and Ken was certainly one, if not the best. Having cut his teeth some years earlier as a control reporter, his prowess in often raising the stakes when regulation became problematic spoke volumes. Whilst the odd spurious comment may have been directed towards Ken, his overall ability left others with some catching up to do. Little did I know that a couple of years later when I was courting a girl who is now my wife, I learned that she lived a couple of hundred yards from Ken and his wife, and with her friend used to baby-sit for them in her younger days. Almost 40 years later and not having seen or heard of him since those halcyon days, I rang Ken at his home in Sawley, where he had moved from nearby Long Eaton, to ask him to refresh my memory regarding a signalling issue at Sheet Stores. Whilst he couldn't be positive about the suggestion that Lock Lane could release the starting signal without the requisite 'Line clear', it was a fact in the reverse direction. Indeed, Ken went on to say that a similar situation applied from Attenborough Junction and Station signal boxes. After putting the world to rights and without any prompting from me, he then recalled those early evenings with Sid on the Wellingborough-Chaddesden, he had forgotten the name of his fireman.

Ray Collins, a Controller at Leicester took this photograph of the Wellingborough-Chaddesden freight at Burton Latimer in 1959 with its usual LMS Class 8F 2-8-0, here No. 48403. This was always a highlight on the late turn at Sheet Stores.

Ray Collins

This was all the more pleasing as, being a relief man, he had only brief interludes at Sheet Stores but witnessed the running of the freight from other locations. I detected a semblance of gratification as those reminiscences came flooding back.

During our conversation Ken told me that in addition to working those in the Trent area, he signed for the signal boxes from Codnor Park on the Erewash Valley to Hathern; on my reckoning this amounted to some 30 relieving points. He also recalled the time when the 3 p.m. Cricklewood-Derby St. Mary's milk empties came to grief at Sheet Stores. Doug Lawson was the signalman, Ken being on the late turn at Ratcliffe Junction. It was early evening and foggy, the Manchester express had gone by and the milk empties then came down the goods line from Trent Junction to follow the Bradford express from Sheet Stores.

When the signals were cleared for the express, the driver of the milk empties for whatever reason took this as his signal, promptly ran through the stop blocks and some way down the embankment. Another story which did the rounds was where Doug, supposedly to clip up the points, initially placed the point clip on top of the rail.

One event from the winter timetable of 1958 remains in my memory; the Sunday 5.15 p.m. from Manchester (London Road) to London was diverted from Euston to St. Pancras in order to relieve pressure on the West Coast line during weekend occupations in connection with electrification. Longsight (9A) provided the necessary Class '7P' motive power and the train was routed via Kidsgrove and then over the North Stafford line to Stenson Junction; there it took the branch line to Sheet Stores Junction and then up the Midland Main Line to St. Pancras. The following year saw certain other Manchester expresses on the L.N.W.R. diverted to and from St. Pancras including the overnights. Apart from the odd ballast train on Sundays, the branch line between Stenson Junction and Sheet Stores Junction would be clear. However, during the week it was totally different and frantic efforts were made to clear the branch for the passage of the 12 noon from Manchester London Road. Freight trains on occasions had to be shunted

Manchester-St. Pancras express hauled by a commendably clean "Jubilee" Class 4-6-0 No. 45587 'Baroda' passing Trent Junction in September 1960. A Longsight (9A) engine, this is probably the 12 noon from Manchester London Road, which, with others had been diverted over the Midland Main Line owing to electrification work on the Western Lines.
J.A. Wade

out of the way for the express that was due at Sheet Stores at 2.25 p.m., it was then allowed just over two hours to cover the 119½ miles to St. Pancras. It came from the branch at 15mph; I would open the window and if the train was late, intimate to the driver by how many minutes. On checking his pocket watch, and with the usual broad grin and a full head of steam, up would go the regulator and away he stormed. In the reverse direction the 1.55 p.m. from St. Pancras was also booked over the Castle Donington route due into Manchester London Road at 6.33 p.m, before later being diverted to Victoria arriving at 7. 1 p.m., however, by using the direct 2.25 p.m. St. Pancras-Manchester Central folk could arrive at 6.9 p.m.

I will always be eternally grateful to my mother not only for her continued support, but also for acting as my early morning alarm call. In those days the BBC didn't broadcast through the night, and when on the early shift I was awakened by an American Forces Network programme from Germany called Hilly Billy Revelry (or some similar title). This was a country and western half hour with records by legendary singers Hank Locklin, Hank Williams, Patsy Cline and Johnny Cash to name but a few. Starting at 5 a.m. during the winter months, the reception was very good; whilst in the summer an hour later it was less so.

* * *

Although freight trains had timetabled paths in the same way as passenger and parcels trains, bad weather conditions often hindered their progress. Fog was a prime cause of delay particularly whenever double block working was being resorted to. Most freight trains that had commenced their journey at Toton, Beeston, Nottingham and Chaddesden could be expected to run reasonably near to their booked time, whilst the afternoon Wellingborough-Chaddesden invariably ran ahead of schedule. Empty wagon trains from various locations often ran late and had to take their chance with others.

Express freight services running under Class 'C' and partially fitted ones with 'D' and 'E' headcodes were generally good timekeepers. The nightly Ancoats-London Class 'C', often produced one of the four named Stanier Class '5's, two of which were transferred to Newton Heath from St. Rollox and still sporting the enlarged numerals. It was the only freight train other than the Sheet Stores trip to be booked via the North Curve from Sawley Junction and effected relief at Trent station by a Toton traincrew. The plethora of junctions around Trent, often had trainspotters gnashing their teeth; they're being no way that all trains could be viewed. The endless procession of freight trains from the high speed 'Condor' to the humble pick-up often yielded locomotives from far off depots. Unfortunately for the majority, apart from the Leicester-Carlisle and Somers Town-Masborough, the other fast freights ran during the night, e.g. Attercliffe-Birmingham, Carlisle-Leicester, Carlton-Leicester, Dringhouses-Lawley Street, Edgehill-Nottingham, Glasgow (Buchanan Street)-St. Pancras, Greenhill-Wilhampstead (motor cars), Bathgate-Luton (empties), Hurlford-Brent, Moston-Brent, Nottingham-Bristol, Rowsley-London, Stourton-St. Pancras and not forgetting the Carlisle-Cricklewood Milk (466) which had equal regulation standing to that of an express.

Brand spanking new, BR Sulzer Type '4' D57 temporarily uprated from 2,500hp to 2,750hp on loan to Toton passing through Trent with a train of 21 ton vacuum fitted wagons from Castle Donington power station to Langley Mill, circa 1961.

Coal trains from Toton and returning empty wagons to Toton and Beeston ran throughout the day and night. Stone trains operated during the day from the Northamptonshire ore fields, most having loose-coupled iron-ore tipplers that were not vacuum fitted. Initially worked by Stanier Class 8F and the renowned Beyer-Garratts (2-6-6-2) before they were ousted by the advent of the BR Standard Class 9Fs. Services of note were: – Ashwell-Frodingham, Corby-Glazebrook, Glendon-Burslem, Storefield-York and Wellingborough-Grange, the returning empty iron-ore tipplers conveyed on the 07.30 Toton-Pain's Siding and the Clay Cross-Wellingborough. Strangely enough when the original 10 'Peak' diesel locomotives were displaced off the Western Lines and allocated to Toton in 1962, often a brake tender was attached to provide additional brake-force.

A periodic shipment of Spanish ore was always guaranteed to provide a varied selection of motive power from depots in the northwest. The commodity was extremely heavy and each train was limited to twenty-six non-fitted iron ore tippler wagons, running from Birkenhead to Stanton Gate for the BSC works, via Crewe and the North Stafford line. This influx of locomotives from unbalanced workings no doubt supplemented Toton's allocation at the time. On the theme of unbalanced locomotive workings, most Monday mornings would see a cavalcade of five locomotives coupled together, all in steam, running from the Birmingham division Saltley/Bescot to Toton.

* * *

The Signal and Telegraph Department was located at Trent station. Many of us at some time or another have inadvertently dropped the telephone, resulting in the bakelite being chipped or broken. Bob Naylor and Billy Powell would attend to this, track circuit failures and any problems associated with the block signalling equipment. On the mechanical front, where difficulty was experienced with point detection and signals, Fred Astle and his team would respond. Fred almost wanted a written report on the matter before he would start work.

I had no real desire to be a signalman, although I had enjoyed the opportunity in my latter school days of visiting and partaking in the operation of five signal boxes. Diversification was the order of the day and, after failing to meet the required colour vision level

THE BRITISH TRANSPORT COMMISSION

SYLLABUS OF EXAMINATION FOR APPLICANTS
FOR APPOINTMENT AS CLERKS.
(Common to all Departments).

1. ENGLISH – Writing from dictation. Spelling. Meaning of words. Correction of sentences. Composition. Paraphrasing.

2. GEOGRAPHY & GENERAL KNOWLEDGE – Geography of Great Britain on general knowledge lines: e.g. elementary knowledge of physical geography; holiday resorts and ports with their broad geographical situation; industries, architectural features etc. and the towns with which they are associated.

   Prominent personalities – the positions they occupy in current affairs, or the science, industry, profession etc. in connection with which their names have become known. Elementary Post Office and banking regulations for the general public; e.g. addressing envelopes, the uses of postal orders and cheques.

   Well-known characters of fiction, titles of books, and authors.

3. ARITHMETIC – Addition, Subtraction, multiplication and division. British money and weights. Fractions, (Alternative questions will be set). Averages, Proportion, Practice, Percentage, Profit and Loss, Simple Interest.

for the footplate grade, knew that control-reporting duties were the starting platform for other opportunities that would become available. I submitted an application to transfer to the clerical staff and a period of time elapsed before sitting the entrance examination in my own time. Early in 1960, Stan Burchell, a Telegraph Clerk at Trent, moved on promotion to Controller in the Line Managers Office at Derby, being closely followed by John Hardaker who went to a similar position in the Nottingham Control Office. The Rest Day Relief clerk David Shaw took the vacancy left by Burchell and I subsequently filled the other vacancy.

*   *   *

In 1961 under the name of Warren Smith, Tony Smith, the stationmaster at Trent penned an article for Trains Illustrated, describing 'The problems of train regulation – a study of operation at Trent'. This was an in-depth look at the movement and signalling of trains through the plethora of junctions, supplemented by a selection of his photographs. By this time he had moved on with spells at Sheffield, Wolverhampton and Derby, before I met up with him again in 1978. He was Passenger Officer in the Divisional Manager's Office at Bristol when I moved to Laira (Plymouth) as Movements Supervisor. Tony fell foul of the higher echelons at Western Regional Headquarters at Paddington, often being accused of running a 'Bristol private railway'. More of this in a future edition.

In 1996 I wrote to Tony at his home on the Isle of Arran to ask him about the gradient profile between Trent South and Sheet Stores and the location of a signal. He replied to both queries and added, "I took many railway photos at Trent and although several were inadvertently destroyed (or the negatives were) and O.S. Nock lost some; I've still quite a good selection left. If you ever get round to writing about Trent and are looking for any pictures I'll see what printable ones are left."

*   *   *

"Well I'll go to Trent", and there I was, back after three years. I would spend a further six years at the station – in retrospect, a few wasted ones. Thereafter, the five years in Control were undoubtedly the highlight of a 39-year railway career.

On refection the year spent on the relief, together with the two years at Sheet Stores had many highlights, working with a cross section of signalmen whose temperaments varied as often as the weather. How refreshing it was to have Norman Earl, the rest day relief signalman in charge whose philosophy was "give 'em a run"! There were others of course including the regular signalmen who showed scant regard to the fact that they were there to run and regulate trains, on occasions showed negativity to regulating and decision making, some preferring to put the onus onto the Control Office.

At some junctions you would here the signalman calling Control; "I've got so-and-so coming on the branch and such-and-such on the main, which shall I run first?" It was often necessary to persuade the signalmen to make more decisions themselves.

Harking back to those halcyon days at Toton Centre and the redoubtable Bill Butler, who used to pull the leg of Stan Salmon the Old Bank shunter unmercifully, referring to him as 'Inspector'? That, along with his often-daily tirade against enginemen made for a very interesting period, tantamount to a baptism of fire. Then, for the following two weeks sanity prevailed in the shape of Jimmy Trigger and George Bailey.

The sight of "Johnny the Lamp" always smiling even in the harshest of weather conditions, often resembling a snowman. Dear old Arthur Higginbottom, whose pocket watch was always a different time from the clock in the signal box. The Welsh wizard Alfie Jones, in addition to his breeches backside hanging out his unlaced shoes sadly in need of a clean, the inane jabbering in that 'foreign' language. Farmer Williams in the field opposite shooting rabbits in the sight of the headlights of his tractor. 'One arm' Jack Stevens, signalman at Sawley Junction whose power when pulling the distant signal made those screw tops dance. The deep tones of Freddie Pratt when asking, "any more please um?" Fred Astle signal & telegraph department, a problem with detection or a broken signal wire – cause mismanagement! The usual Monday morning cavalcade of five unbalanced steam locomotives returning from Saltley to Toton m.p.d. On the late turn the eagerly awaited running of the Wellingborough-Chaddesden freight.

*   *   *

Listening to some of the stories told by the signalmen on the omnibus telephone circuit. Bill Stringer at Borrowash, who temporarily secured the door on the platelayers hut, with the personnel inside and promptly placed a tile on top of the smoking chimney, George Burton a platelayer from the Ratcliffe length, dodging the cup full of water aimed at him when on his way home cycling down the path at the back of the 'box. The mad scramble each lunchtime to clear the branch of freight trains for the passage of the 12 noon Manchester London Road – St Pancras, one of a number of expresses diverted in connection with the Western Lines electrification scheme. Another lighter moment was the late afternoon/early evening commuter service from Nottingham, bringing home the office/shop assistants to Sawley Junction. Those girls would wave feverishly at most of the signal boxes en-route, doubtless hoping and receiving a response in return.

Watching the minutes tick by as the early morning freights for the Castle Donington branch fought to regain their footing on the rise from Trent South, The eerie silence during those peasouper fogs, wondering how long it would be before the train lit up the track circuit. What a relief it was to have a fogsignalman on duty, even more appreciated by the enginemen.

Three
"Well I'll Go to Trent!"

Trent station could be a most inhospitable place; biting north/north easterly winds that chilled the marrow to the bone, the hardiest of individuals would seek shelter in the waiting rooms or solace in the refreshment room, when open. As mentioned earlier the dense pea-souper fogs effaced all sounds and trains would arrive in the platform unannounced. During an offbeat moment whilst participating in the present day card school at the Railway Inn at Sawley, during conversation it came to light that Alan Foster, a close friend, reminded me that he delivered the newspapers to the bookstall at the station in the mid 1950s. The bookstall however had long since disappeared on my arrival at Trent.

Two views of Trent station.
George Bailey

After an initial spell training and gaining knowledge of booking office duties, of which I recall the month-end balance being rather onerous, I was dispatched to the telegraph office at Nottingham Midland station to learn the Morse code. Jimmy Mann was in charge there with various clerks, 'The Bishop' who always sported a rose in his lapel, Jack Porter, and another who regaled himself by pilfering the delivery of milk from doorsteps. There, literally for days on end, I sat in awe, mesmerised at the speed of the exchanges between the operator of the two pedal instruments and his opposite number at the Kettering telegraph office, could any of this make sense?

For a number of weeks there appeared little if any progress was being made, it certainly took some digesting. Eventually, Bert Frost came to pass me out, sending messages from the telegraph office at Nottingham Victoria, and, with more than a little help from one of the clerks, I struggled through. Obviously with more practice when back at Trent the more competent I became. Even so I was never as proficient as I would have hoped for, there wasn't a problem in receiving train reports over the system as one became familiar with the timetabled trains reporting numbers, and sending was relatively straightforward. The difficulty I had together with the other clerks was the sporadic receiving of telegrams (messages), and although the sender was requested to send the message slowly, some were less than considerate.

Wires (messages) were also dictated over the telephone, most being received from the telegraph office at Derby for onward transmission to various outlets in the local area. Those to the Toton Yard Master's Office, and also to the Motive Power Depot could be extremely lengthy and of course all had to be handwritten, which was extremely time consuming. They would range from temporary speed restrictions being imposed, relaxed, or not taking place, special 'out-of-gauge' train movements and the acknowledgement of special traffic notices. Locomotives that were out of service with shopping proposals being submitted always proved interesting reading. All in all it was a far cry from today's sophisticated state of the art computer systems.

Of the two instruments in the telegraph office, each equipped with two pedals and two sounders, (I'm not sure as to whether I could have mastered the single needle system) one linked Trent with Chesterfield and Masborough (Rotherham), the other Leicester, Nottingham, Chesterfield and Sheffield.

All had their own call signs using the Morse code, dots and dashes alphabet, Trent being 'H' four dots. Trains that took the Erewash Valley route, the up 'Thames-Clyde Express' for example, when passing Chesterfield accounted for reporting to no fewer than fourteen signal boxes between Pye Bridge Junction and Loughborough. Class 1 and 3 trains were reported into the office when passing Melton Mowbray and Millers Dale, also Class 2 when leaving Derby and later on departure from Nottingham, all being disseminated to the respective signal boxes. Express freight services (fully-fitted and partially-fitted) running under Class C & D conditions were also reported both at, and to strategic points, some often having parity with local passenger trains. Interestingly enough, the Carlisle to Cricklewood milk train, reporting No. 466 that passed through Trent at around 1.15 a.m. and hauled by a Holbeck 'Jubilee' would even have priority if running slightly behind time, over the 9.30 p.m. Bradford Forster Square-St. Pancras express from Trent Junction. All the reports were logged and periodically a census was undertaken on the number received and transmitted over a twenty-four hour period. Trent station was manned with a foreman on each shift, two porters on early and late turn, supplemented by a parcels porter, with one porter on the night turn. The ticket barrier was staffed on the early and late turns from where a platform ticket could be issued, or, a ticket to take to the booking office to purchase a ticket to travel. Tom Blakeman, his wife and three daughters had charge of the refreshment room; never particularly busy, although no doubt much appreciated by some passengers when subjected to late running services or severed connections.

Each evening around six-thirty the booking office closed, the telegraph clerks with a £4 float then undertook these duties. The porters assisted in transferring the two large ticket racks together with the requisite bookwork between the two offices. No sooner had this move taken place than the parcels traffic would begin to arrive. Jones & Strouds -where I spent five months before joining the railway- and Pressac, whose components were extremely weighty, both sent heavy packages. The reason that, out of the way Trent was used in preference to nearby Sawley Junction or Long Eaton stations was the greater diversity of services from there.

The travel facilities enjoyed by railway staff enabled those so inclined to make the maximum use of the five free passes per year, and whereas only one 'foreign' free ticket was allowed a few years earlier, the relaxation then resulted in greater diversification. Together with unlimited privilege tickets, where a return journey was half the publicised single fare. It was the general rule to have the free tickets made out to commence at, or in the vicinity of your local station. I saw this however as being restrictive, hence the idea of using the south coast as the starting point to maximise their usage. Various itineraries were contemplated, including French Ports on one occasion, but after sampling Brighton once, I settled on Weymouth and Bournemouth where 'Merchant Navy' and 'West Country' Pacifics still held sway. Any recognised routing could be undertaken which would allow travel to Scotland to be made via the East Coast, West Coast and the Midland lines, or a combination of all three. To make the most of this facility the dating of the tickets was crucial, they had to overlap.

BRITISH RAILWAYS/LONDON TRANSPORT			Request Form for Privilege Ticket/s (Not Transferable). B.R.6599/11		
Name and Initials of Employee (Active or Retired) or Widow M..(Block letters)					
	Male	Female	CLASS (in words)	SINGLE OR RETURN	
SELF					
WIFE*			FROM		
CHILDREN:- 3 and under 15 years of age (subject to income limit)			TO		
15 years of age and under 21 (subject to income limit)			No/s of Ticket/s Issued		Initials of Booking Clerk.
21 years of age or over (wholly dependent)					

*Cross out when issued under authority to dependent female relative acting as housekeeper and insert "HOUSEKEEPER". I hereby apply for ticket/s as above (subject to the Regulations and Conditions printed on the Application Form for Privilege Ticket Identity Cards) and declare that it is/they are for the use of the person/s above mentioned.

Signed.. Grade .... IDENTITY CARD/S ....

Department .... LETTERS AND ....

Employed at... Region............................ NUMBERS ....

IMPORTANT—THIS FORM MUST BE COMPLETED IN INK

Sid Shelton, a dour individual and a habitual smoker was the Chief Booking Clerk, it was his responsibility to countersign the privilege ticket application forms. These had to show the details of the journeys to be undertaken and a register was held in the booking office. A year or so later Sid left Trent, I'm not sure whether he moved to Attenborough station nearer to where he resided, but that effectively meant that the booking office duties would soon be amalgamated permanently and undertaken round the clock by the telegraph clerks. Around 8.30 a.m. one morning, I well remember after handing over to the Booking clerk, he came back a short time later advising me that there was a shortfall in cash compared with the tickets sold that morning. Racking my brain, it was a while before I could determine how it might have occurred. After a degree of soul searching I came to the conclusion that the error materialised when a Sister from the nearby convent booked a day return to St. Pancras at a cost of twenty-seven shillings – £1.35p today. A £5 note was tendered and the lady was given too much change in coins. The fact that the loss may have gone to a good cause made it no less acceptable.

* * *

Quite often, a somewhat liberal view was taken of the permanent 15 m.p.h. speed restriction through Trent station particularly on the down road. None more so than British Railways fastest freight train, the 'Condor', with its 27 platefit wagons making staccato overtures on the jointed track and the Luton-Bathgate motor car train to name but two.

Eastern Region B1 4-6-0 No. 61325 departing Trent station with the 7.0 a.m. Cleethorpes-Birmingham on 4th March 1959. During summer Saturdays the service was extended to Bournemouth and later to Sidmouth and Exmouth. A freight train from Beeston stands on the goods line awaiting a path.
Tony Smith

Another train that often-showed scant regard for the mandatory speed restriction was the down 'Thames-Clyde Express' until a station stop was introduced in late 1962.

This prestigious train, 'The Thames-Clyde Express', in the summer months a relief train ran from Glasgow St. Enoch to St. Pancras on Mondays, Fridays and Saturdays some fifteen minutes ahead of the main train. In the reverse direction a relief train ran as far as Sheffield on Mondays, Fridays and Saturdays, and was extended to Glasgow on peak summer Saturdays. Another long distance express was the 7 a.m. Cleethorpes-Birmingham New Street hauled by its customary Eastern Region Class 'B1' 4-6-0, returning with the afternoon working. In the late 1950s the train was extended to Bournemouth on a summer Saturday and in the early 1960s conveyed through coaches to Sidmouth and Exmouth.

* * *

In addition to the two telegraph instruments, the concentrator housed seven telephone circuits primarily used for train reporting to signal boxes, and the receiving and transmitting of telegrams, an eighth line connected to the stationmaster. The GPO line (Long Eaton 2070) where callers could be connected via a mini exchange to the stationmaster, permanent way office, booking office and later the district signalman's office when transferred from Long Eaton station. The DSI in those days was Jim Barnes; he remained at Trent with his assistant until the power signal box came on stream in 1969. From then

When travelling overnight, the Royal Train on occasions was stabled on the north-curve between Trent Station North Junction and Sawley Junction amid tight security, on a need to know basis. Here the Sheet Stores trip is on its way to Chaddesden meandering along with Midland Class 4F 0-6-0 No. 44195 on 18th June.
Tony Smith

he moved to Toton as a Quality Services Supervisor in the old Toton Centre signal box. Jim was known as Lord Cuff, owing to the amount of shirtsleeve protruding below his jacket sleeve. In his days at Trent he was addressed as Mr. Barnes, and in later years when I relieved him as QSS he told me I could call him 'Sir'!

As mentioned earlier, the only freight trains timetabled to run over the North Curve between Trent Station North Junction and Sawley Junction were the Sheet Stores trip

and the Class 'C' Ancoats-London. Gone were the days when engines fresh off overhaul at Derby Locomotive Works ran on test via Chaddesden and the North Curve, although the diesel multiple units built at the Derby Litchurch Lane Works in the 1950s also utilised this route when returning after trials on the Churnet Valley line. On the passenger front all that remained in the early 1960s were the 11.50 p.m. St. Pancras to Leeds City, which conveyed sleeping cars and afforded a connection to Nottingham by changing at Trent and the 9.2 p.m. (SO) Bradford Forster Square to St. Pancras. This service also catered for passengers leaving Nottingham at 11.55 p.m. wishing to travel back to Loughborough and Leicester after a night out. One foreman, not on my shift I hasten to add, seized on the opportunity of having couples with an hour to wait, by preparing a 'waiting' room secreted at the far end of the platform with a large fire, blinds drawn, he obviously derided some pleasure from his vantage point looking in through a custom made peephole.

For express and parcel trains that called at Trent, a train report slip (TR) was completed by the station foreman:

Train reporting No.

Arrival and departure times,

Class of locomotive,

Tonnage,

Loading L= light Q= normal Y=full Z = standing/full.

This information was then given over to the Line Managers Office at Derby; this was the Divisional Control as distinct from the District Control Office. It was whilst tendering this information that I first came across Ken McLaughlin who was one of the controllers. Ginger as he was known (after his beard) could be relied upon to obtain tickets for all manner of international football matches at Wembley.

He actually brought out to Trent station a couple of tickets for the game between England and Portugal when the great Eusebio turned out for the visitors. A relief signalman, Barry Richardson – whose 'box lad I had been on occasions – accompanied me to the match, extremely enjoyable, apart from the 3 a.m. arrival time back at Trent.

Strange when talking to those controllers how the picture formulated looks nothing like them. Another controller out of the LMO I met 'blind' was Ron (Dad) Adams and we arranged to meet at Wollaton Hall (Nottingham) where a photographic exhibition of steam locomotives was being held. Stan Edge in the same office always came across as tired and irritable, although I'm sure that he wasn't, I had to smile when he answered the telephone with his rather dry and elongated 'ello-o-o-o-o. The doyen of the shift was Jack Galletley, Deputy Chief Controller, whose mild manner and politeness endeared him to many, I very much regret never having met him personally. On the late turn he would ring me to enquire the whereabouts of the 'Thames-Clyde Express' and also its relief train when running.

During our conversations – on occasions he would answer the telephone when I was to give over the details of a TR – Jack often told me that he would not be satisfied until I was sitting alongside him in the LMO at Derby. A few years later I shared those sentiments during an interview with J.A.McEvoy, Divisional Operating Superintendent at Nottingham, for the position of Assistant Passenger Controller at Leicester. It might have been purely coincidental that I was the successful applicant. Tony Smith had left Trent for pastures new before I was ensconced as telegraph clerk and there were a variety of relief stationmasters covering the vacancy. George Hornbuckle who was a reasonable

---

The Thames-Clyde Express
9.20 a.m. Glasgow St. Enoch-St. Pancras
Friday 24th March 1961

With BR/Sulzer Type '4' diesel locomotives in charge of many Midland Main Line express trains at the time it was pleasing to see the performance of steam power on this train despite the late running. Seldom did the Leeds (Holbeck) Royal Scots work south from Leeds to London, on this particular day the enginemen put up a very spirited performance. All of the arrears being recouped, with an arrival time in London one minute early.

Leeds	25 late.
Cudworth	18 late.
Sheffield	14 late.
Chesterfield	13 late.
Pye Bridge	15 late 2 minutes lost owing to p.way check at Hasland.
Trent	11 late.
Loughborough	10 late.
Leicester	6 late.
Kettering	2 late.
St. Pancras	1 minute before time.

Engine – Class 7P 4-6-0 No.46113 'Cameronian'
Load – Ten-coaches
The details obtained from the Line Managers Office at Derby.

---

cricketer, David Winkle who later moved to Derby as Chief Inspector before leaving the railway to keep a cycle shop at Blackpool, and Frank Read who I would confer with a few years later when working in the Nottingham Control Office.

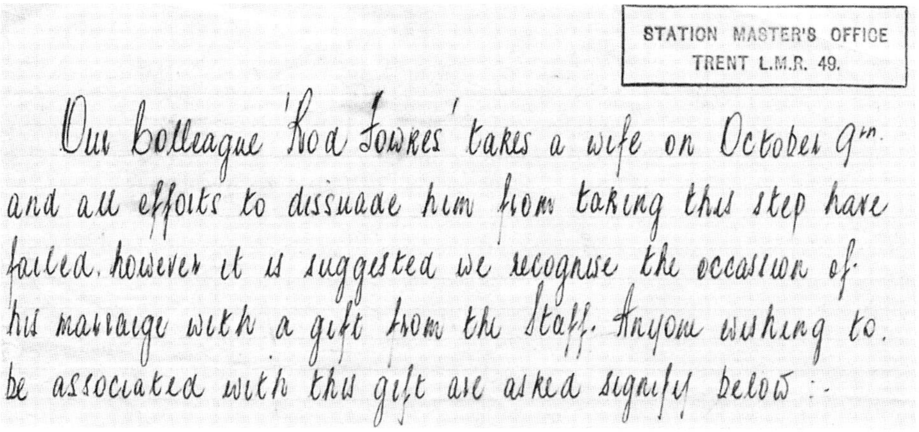

STATION MASTER'S OFFICE
TRENT L.M.R. 49.

Our colleague 'Rod Towner' takes a wife on October 9th. and all efforts to dissuade him from taking this step have failed. however it is suggested we recognise the occasion of his marriage with a gift from the staff. Anyone wishing to be associated with this gift are asked signify below :-

Frank Read was relief Station-master on the run up to my wedding and drafted the following memo ...

*   *   *

The 'Midland Pullman' made its debut in public service on 4th July 1960, running between Manchester Central leaving at 8.50 a.m. calling at Cheadle Heath only and arriving St. Pancras at 12.3 p.m. Returning from St. Pancras at 6.10 p.m. and reaching

The Midland Pullman having left Nottingham Midland at 3.45pm for St. Pancras is routed through the 3rd up passenger line at Trent, *circa* 1961.
George Bailey

Manchester Central at 9.21 p.m. again calling only at Cheadle Heath. It was at the time the fastest rail service ever offered between the two cities; unusually it avoided Derby by taking the route through Chaddesden. Not long after its introduction the departure time was brought forward to 7.45 a.m. to give an earlier arrival in the capital of 11 a.m. The following year after long protracted discussions and bitter union opposition, a mid-day Midland Pullman service was augmented leaving St. Pancras at 11.20 a.m. to Nottingham. There, it was fully cleaned returning at 3.45 p.m. back to London for its 6.10 departure.

*   *   *

An overnight Leeds-Bedford parcels train detached its rearmost van in the up platform just after half-past three, to be picked up within the hour by the 3.57 a.m. Derby-Nottingham parcels train. During the time that the van occupied the platform line other trains were routed through the 3rd up passenger line. As a matter of interest the up and down 2nd passenger lines were seldom used except by short trains or light engines that might be waiting for a path, the distant signals for these lines could not be worked and were fixed at caution.

*   *   *

In December 1960, the swollen River Erewash washed away a culvert at Attenborough Junction on the Derby-Nottingham line, which remained closed for the next five days. Throughout this period the Derby-Nottingham DMU service was diverted to Leicester using the north curve at Trent, with a bus service affording connections between Sawley Junction and Attenborough. A special bus service also operated between the Midland station at Derby and Friargate station to connect into the ex-G.N. route trains to Nottingham Victoria. Other trains were diverted from Nottingham to run via Radford and Trowell where a shuttle DMU ran to and from Long Eaton. A couple of unusual workings involved the 4.55 p.m. Birmingham-Cleethorpes, with the usual 'B1' 4-6-0, it took the Erewash Valley route as far as Trowell where another 'B1' attached to the rear and continued via Radford onto Nottingham. The 8.1 p.m. 'mail' from Lincoln to Tamworth was diverted over the Trowell branch, then via Butterley to Ambergate and Derby.

Although a fully-fledged Telegraph Clerk, I was occasionally called upon for control-reporting duties at both Sheet Stores and Trent South when staff in the wages grade could not be found to work a turn for whatever reason. In addition I was also requested to cover a shortage at Draycott & Breaston station on porter's duties. This usually coincided with my night turn and I undertook this duty until 10 a.m., as living close by it was no hardship. Still working at the station was wee George Mellors; it was he who was instrumental in my joining the railway some years earlier. A couple of colourful characters at Trent station were Arthur Roulstone and Jim Simpson, both porters. Arthur's nickname was Fangio (shortened even further to Fan) after the Argentine racing driver whom he waxed lyrical over. He was a very cheerful chap, slightly hard of hearing, forever whistling and busying himself around the station, sweeping, dusting and seldom still. Fan lived at Draycott and when we were both on the early shift he would call at my house and we cycled to work together. Whilst the dawn chorus may be acceptable to most, his incessant whistling together with a penetrating voice was far from being appropriate at five o'clock in the morning. Nevertheless he was a very sincere and conscientious man, this led to some of his colleagues not pulling their weight on cleaning duties, knowing full well that Fan would always respond without question. Jim was referred to as 'Doctor' Simpson, a title derived from his perception of the healing processes, whereby most ills could be cured by regular visits to the small room, a belief he expounded liberally. Jim spent many hours in the Victoria Inn run by Johnny Phipps, a hundred yards or so from his home. His wife was out most of the time on her rounds doing good for others, leaving Jim on his own for long periods and he obviously found solace at the Vic. Jim defended his wife admirably. One day in the company of 'Daddy' Dearman, a relief stationmaster, with Arthur (Fan) Roulstone looking on, Jim, who had part of a finger missing was pontificating as usual, said "I wouldn't take five thousand pounds for Gladys", enhancing that with his second and third fingers of his right hand flat against the palm, with the first and fourth out straight. Mr. Dearman asked, "Is that your wife Jim?" which came the reply, "My second wife!" Well, the look on the face of Fan spoke volumes, and mumbled that he wouldn't give five pence for Gladys. Although he may not have been an authority on radios he did point me in the right direction when looking for a replacement of the one loaned by my sister Jane. Jim had a Roberts radio that he positively enthused about, made by a small family run concern and not available at the major outlets of the time such as Currys and the Co-op. A local retailer in Long Eaton stocked them and I recall paying around £18 for the LW/MW/SW band radio that was equivalent to a fortnight's basic salary. So impressed was Bert Callard the stationmaster, that he also purchased a Roberts radio. These radios are reproduced today at a cost of well over £100. Another of the station porters, Sid Armstrong who was getting on in years, asked me one day if I would help him to pick pears off his very large tree. I duly obliged and was rewarded with a bag of pears. Whilst in conversation in his front room I happened to pass comment on a wall clock. To my amazement he immediately offered it to me, after expressing my appreciation I laid the four-foot Vienna clock over the handlebars of my bicycle and walked the couple of miles home. It still adorns my dining room.

Eric Smith, the timekeeper in the permanent way office, was perceived by many as being an artist, not however the drawing or painting type. Very often he would pop his head round the door around lunchtime to say he was going for a haircut which entailed walking down the path to Long Eaton and afterwards to the nearest hostelry. One day on the early turn I was relieved at 12.45 p.m. I met Eric at the Railway Inn and by closing time at three o'clock was very much the worse for wear. The two miles cycling home seemed like an eternity with a few tumbles, the abrasions and torn trousers bearing testi-

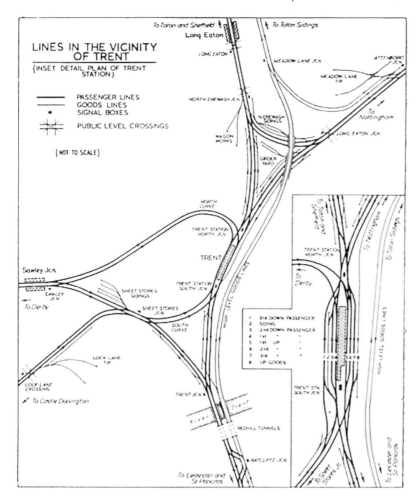

mony. Sheepishly, I staggered in not knowing whether or not I could stomach any dinner.

The plethora of junctions around the Trent triangle often had train spotters gnashing their teeth, there being no way that the numbers of all engines could be seen. Some would position themselves on the station with the requisite plat-form ticket, often uttering groans as an express tore by between Sheet Stores and Trent Junctions. Nonetheless there were the often-endless procession of mineral trains emanating from Toton sidings rattling by on the high-level goods line to the Stewart & Lloyds steelworks at Corby, Wellingborough and Brent, where London had an insa-tiable appetite for coal. In addition there were coal trains going towards the Castle Donington branch from both Beeston and Toton with the returning trains of empties for the collieries that produced a multitude of Midland type locomotives.

Enginemen and guards were con-veyed to and from Toton depot to Trent station by a 'bus'. It wasn't unusual for Nottingham Control to ring up asking to intercept a train crew. They might have been travelling to Kettering or Wellingborough to work a down freight when it was learnt that it was not running. Many of those trains from the south (apart from the empties from the London area) emanated from the ore fields in Northamptonshire. When Toton was on the block, which was quite often, these stone trains were regarded as 'throughs' and would be turned out at either Ratcliffe Junction or Trent Junction to run through the station down the Erewash Valley, instead of standing behind other freight trains on the down high-level goods line that were awaiting acceptance into Toton yard.

* * *

Each location had its characters; Locomotive Inspector Cyril Jones with his jaunty walk was christened Dark Hour by the enginemen and staff at Toton. He would cycle from nearby Long Eaton to Trent station and make his way to either Derby or Nottingham as the case may be. During the intervals waiting for a train he would regale with his footplate experiences. Cyril let me have his completed logbook of runs primarily undertaken on expresses and the odd freight train. On perusing his logs it was interesting to note that double-heading on specific services during 1957 and the first part of 1958 was rife, in particular 10.40 a.m. Bradford Forster Square-St. Pancras from Nottingham and 4.25 p.m. St. Pancras-Manchester Central as far as Derby. The 8.15 a.m. from Nottingham Midland 'Robin Hood' also featured with a pilot engine. Little wonder that the Midland Lines welcomed the transfer of Class 7 'Royal Scot' locomotives for the 1957 winter timetable and the following year the acquisition by Trafford Park of the 'Britannia' Pacifics eliminated almost all of the double-heading unless required for balancing purposes.

Applications to visit Motive Power Depots were seldom declined when submitted through the stationmaster and the staff office, and signalman Barry Richardson accompanied me on one occasion to Aberdeen. However, as regards the depots north of the border, I wrote to the Public Relations and Publicity Officer in Glasgow who always acceded to my many requests over a five-year period. In August 1961, armed with a batch of permits to visit engine sheds in Scotland courtesy of the Public Relations and Publicity Officer in Glasgow, I joined the overnight St. Pancras-Glasgow St. Enoch sleeper train at Derby just after midnight where it had just started raining. After the mandatory diesel change at Leeds City it was then raining heavily and when alighting at Dumfries shortly before half past six, the first engine shed to visit; the rain was incessant. A quick look around and it was back to the station to catch the 7.30 a.m. to Kilmarnock, this was the 11.45 p.m. from Euston hauled by a Stanier Pacific. It was a short walk to Hurlford depot, in the driving rain with only a plastic mackintosh as protection against the elements. The next port of call was the depots at Ayr and then onto Ardrossan. It was now half-past-two, and with the engine shed at Ardrossan in view, the rain still teeming down, the lower parts of my trousers saturated where the rain had run off the plastic mac and shoes full of water, I succumbed to the elements and turned around and made my way to Glasgow. There I had tea and went to a cinema – cannot recollect what was showing – to dry out, sitting in there without socks and shoes on.

Leaving Glasgow St. Enoch on the 9 p.m. to St. Pancras reflecting on a soggy day, socks and trousers still rather wet, further drama lay ahead. Shortly after leaving Kilmarnock the train came to a stand, some time elapsed before the guard came through the train to advise the passengers that the line ahead was impassable owing to flooding. Hardly surprising as there had been no let up throughout the day, the rain at times being torrential. After a lengthy delay the train returned over the ex-G & S.W route and was diverted over the ex-Caledonian line via Beattock to Carlisle. The estimated delay was ninety minutes of which a significant amount of those arrears were recovered on reaching St. Pancras, from where a quick dash over to Paddington for the train to Plymouth and a visit to Laira depot.

I well remember standing in the shadows at Glasgow Central station one evening in the early 1960s, when an Anglo-Scottish express limped into platform 1 considerably behind time. The enginemen were then relieved on arrival and the driver was looking clearly out of sorts and positively dejected. He walked in my direction and on making eye contact I said sympathetically, "You've had difficulties?" The driver then proceeded to tell me that until Carlisle there was no problem mechanically but the steam heating boiler on the Brush Type '4' diesel had packed up. The replacement engine came in the shape of an ailing 'Britannia' Pacific that wouldn't pull Granny off the proverbial. He was obviously extremely concerned for the passengers over their late arrival, and it showed.

In the summer of 1961 we moved house, still in the same village, the property had a long garden that backed onto the Derby canal. We were now able to enjoy a few mod cons, electricity, bringing forth a television, an integral bathroom and toilet, no longer having to traipse down the yard in all weathers and the old tin bath would now be used to collect rainwater.

It would be almost a year later that I had my first camera, a Halina 35x, as a 21st birthday present. It didn't occur to me at the time that a camera should have been a priority certainly when starting out on the railway, however with hindsight it was regrettable that for those first five years I had no photographic collection from those early signalbox installations.

My interest in gardening was enhanced by Lewis Taylor the next-door neighbour who could grow almost anything; he was employed at Derby Locomotive Works until his retirement. I learnt a great deal about horticulture from this man.

A concession enjoyed by some, including myself, was the opportunity to purchase firewood at a reduced rate. Obtained from Beeston Creosote Works it came in the form of off-cuts from sleeper ends before they had been treated. It wasn't policy to leave the fire unattended as the wood had a tendency to spit out as the scorch marks on the carpet bore testimony. Nonetheless it did eke out the coal supply, the slow burning wood when banked up with slack would last for hours. The problem was of getting suitable transport to convey the firewood from Beeston to Breaston. Help was at hand though in the form of the driver who ferried train crews between Toton depot and Trent station. Every fourth week the driver was employed transporting material between local depots and the main workshops at Derby. Wednesday was normally a convenient day to collect the firewood. Needless to say one of the station foreman got wind of this and reported the driver who was interviewed and warned by the D.M.P.S. at Toton.

```
BRITISH  RAILWAYS                        B.R.  8040
............................................................Department,
............................................................Station,
...............................................................19..........
APPLICATION FOR FIREWOOD, ETC.,
       FOR RAILWAY SERVANTS
Name........................................................................
                              ⎧ Shop ..............................
Occupation ...................⎨
                              ⎩ Clock  No..................
Private  Address................................................................
   Delete      ⎧ Delivery required private address
   item not    ⎨ Delivery required at             Station
   applicable  ⎩ I will remove from where now lying
Material........................................................................
Quantity ..................................................... P.T.O
                                        B.R.  8040—Back
Price          s.        d.
Particulars of last ⎧ Date ........................................
     Purchase       ⎨
                    ⎩ Quantity.................................
     I wish to purchase the above mentioned material for
my personal use and not for re-selling to any other person.
I agree that The British Transport Commission shall not be
liable in respect of accident howsoever caused and whether
proving fatal or otherwise which may happen to me whilst upon
Railway premises for the purpose of removing the above
mentioned material.
Signature of Employee..............................................
Certified that applicant is a Servant of the British Transport
Commission.
Signature of Superior Officer....................................
To the ................................................
                                        Station
```

* * *

Shift working today is intrinsically more acceptable than it was in the late 1950s and early 60s. Having said that I noticed a difference on leaving Sheet Stores where the control reporters didn't work the Saturday night turn and there were no Sunday duties. Now at Trent, shift work included weekends. Unless rest day on a Saturday on the late turn this meant that the following week on the early shift was the only weekend free, one week in three. John Baxter who lived in the station house at Sawley crossing and Don Stevenson would be out enjoying themselves while I was at, or preparing to go to work. Shift working was become a bind, I perceived it as being anti-social, impeding friendships, a problem which would manifest itself as time progressed. It didn't get any easier when I met Maureen. Having said that if you choose to be a railwayman there had to be some sacrifices, although at that time it was no less palatable.

Away from work, recreational interests such as football and cricket on the park at Breaston and putting on West Park pending on the seasons were usually interspersed with darts and a game of cards at the pub. Five public houses in Old Sawley were in close proximity to each other and three of those New Inn, (later to be called the Sawley Arms), White Lion and Nags Head were trawled regularly. As in my days at Sheet Stores the Sawley Arms beckoned at lunchtime on Saturdays, it was essential to get in there by a quarter to twelve or risk not participating in the Ku-Can card school. I well remember when on the night shift, asking my mother to call me up at eleven o'clock in order that I could cycle the couple of miles to be installed in the school by mid-day. To this request she would retort, "You want to get your rest m'lad". For a while the late turn in the telegraph office did not start until half past three, which was very convenient.

Despite the forays into Scotland, visiting motive power depots and riding behind steam traction, an entry in my diary in 1963 read: – 'determined to leave the railway, fed up with shift work'. At that time there appeared to be a feeling of isolation when my mates were making plans for the weekend while I was at, or going to work. A contributory factor was that I was now courting. Both John Baxter and myself had now found the company of the opposite sex, by way of the Saturday night dances at the Sawley Community Centre, always putting in a last minute appearance after closing time. That year I went for interviews to a couple of building societies in Nottingham, being called back to one for a second interview, and also to Carters soft drinks firm at Sawley where I was offered the position of clerk, which I declined. On reflection I considered it fortuitous not to have been accepted by either society.

Trips, down south, and north of the border continued apace in 1962. Suddenly the Southern Region with its 'Bullied' and 'Light' Pacifics working to Bournemouth and Weymouth, being the last steam stronghold in the south, were producing spirited performances. The Gresley 'A4' Pacifics displaced off the East Coast main line were enjoying a renaissance on Glasgow-Aberdeen 3hr services. It was a bold step taken by the Scottish Region authorities in the summer to entrust the ex-L.N.E.R. locomotives in the days of steadily increasing dieselisation, and their introduction on the accelerated timetable proved to be the 'A4s' swansong. Obtaining the GPO telephone number of the Shed Foreman at Aberdeen Ferryhill proved extremely beneficial, a rapport developed between us and he was most informative regarding the performance and availability of the 'A4s'.

On 6th December 1963, Stanton Gate was the scene of a fatal accident. The collision between two freight trains occurred at Stanton Gate South Junction at 1.32 a.m. when an up freight, the 10.40 p.m. Class 'C' Leeds-Leicester on the up main line and having passed at least two stop signals at danger, collided at an oblique angle (diagonally) with a down freight. The 1 a.m. Toton-Woodhouse Mill was crossing under clear signals from the No. 2 down goods line over the down and up main lines to the No. 1 down goods line. Damage to both trains and the track was considerable and the front end of BR/Sulzer Type 4 diesel No. D94 on the Leeds-Leicester train was almost totally destroyed; this unfortunately caused the deaths of both driver and second man. The Inspecting Officer concluded that the crew of No. D94, who had spent the first part of their turn of duty on a steam locomotive, had become drowsy in the diesel cab, where the lack of fresh air contrasted with conditions on the footplate of a steam locomotive. He added that the accident would have been prevented had AWS been in situ on the line. The two guards of the freight trains were taken to Nottingham General Hospital with one being detained for observation. The Toton crew on the footplate of the steam engine was unhurt; the fireman was commended in isolating the batteries and fuel supply of the diesel locomotive after the accident, even though he had not

Taken from the
Long Eaton Advertiser.

RAILWAY CRASH

The crash is pictured from the railway footbridge at Stanton Gate.

received training on that type of locomotive. Seven years after its opening in 1862, Trent was the scene of one of the worst railway disasters in the history of the Midland Railway. An excursion train returning from Nottingham Goose Fair had been stopped outside the station when it was struck from the rear by the night mail express. Nine passengers were killed.

The winter of 1963, when Arctic weather conditions caused problems nationwide, there was no let up in the penetrating frosts for weeks on end until the snow arrived accompanied by bitter winds. Snowdrifts blocked many rail routes, water troughs and water columns froze up and steam locomotives that had been stored were pressed back into service. Locally, alongside the footpath between North Erewash Junction and Trent station, the ballast hole had become frozen over.

In the vain attempt to oxygenate the water, it appeared that fishermen, realising the plight of the fish had taken to breaking the ice around the perimeter of Forbes hole. All to no avail and this was where the fish languished. Hundreds of pike, starved of oxygen had made for the bank, now frozen, jaws agape; a harrowing site and the stench was awful. David Shaw reminded me that during this cold snap drinking water had to be sourced in, as there was no water at Trent station.

There was much work for the permanent-way staff in snow sweeping duties; the station staffs was also kept busy tending the braziers at the water columns around the station.

*   *   *

On 14th May 1964, Royalty paid a visit to the East Midlands. A portion was detached in the platform off the rear of the 11.50 p.m. St. Pancras-Leeds City which was hauled by splendidly turned out BR/Sulzer Type '2' diesels Nos. D7588/89 Stanier Class '5' locomotive, No. 44918 then hauled the detachment onto the North Curve for stabling whilst another Black '5' No. 45464 was attached on the rear. Special instructions were issued on 'a need to know basis' in connection with the working of Royal trains and were given code words – 'Grove' was used when the Reigning Monarch was aboard and 'Deepdene' for other members of the Royal family.

*   *   *

Having transferred to the salaried staff in 1960, I did not, for whatever reason join the Transport Salaried Staff Association until five years later. Up to that point I had been a member of the National Union of Railwaymen, and anyone relinquishing membership of that union was viewed very seriously, as I was to find out. One Sunday lunchtime at my local, the Navigation Inn at Breaston, with the domino school well under way, Ben, the landlord popped his head round the bar, "Rod, there's a fellow outside would like to speak to you". I asked Ben who it was, what did he want, why didn't he come in? He didn't know. On finishing the game of dominos and getting someone else to play my next hand I went outside to meet this mystery man. He turned out to be Walter Killingback a goods guard at Toton, he was a representative of the NUR who had sent him to see me regarding my leaving the union. After being interrogated as to my reasons for leaving the NUR, I informed him that I had transferred to the TSSA, which was more in keeping with salaried matters. Furthermore, I objected to this intrusion of my leisure time, so, bugger-off! How did he manage to locate me at the Navigation Inn? Well, he had been to my home and mother had unwittingly told him where I could be found. Walter Killingback could be troublesome individual, as I would find out some years later when at Toton in my role as supervisor.

The movement of condemned steam locomotives to various scrap-yards around the system had begun in earnest a few years earlier.

However, not all steam engines were broken up in private sidings. For example on 17/18 March 1964 rebuilt 'Patriot' No. 45536 'Private W. Wood, V.C.' and 'Jubilees' Nos. 45576 'Bombay', 45583 'Hogue', and 45725 'Repulse' were hauled from Staveley M.P.D. to Crewe Works.

J. Cashmore Ltd. at Great Bridge possibly had an affection for the 'Jubilee' class amongst others, as no fewer than nine of these locomotives were programmed into the yard during November, December and January:

16/11/64.	45579 'Punjab'		ex Trafford Park M.P.D.
20/11/64.	45564 'New South Wales'		ex Nottingham M.P.D.
20/11/64.	45631 'Tanganyika'		ex Saltley M.P.D.
04/12/64.	45557 'New Brunswick'	45561 'Saskatchewan'	
	45611 'Hong Kong'	45622 'Nyasaland'	ex Derby M.P.D.
04/01/65.	45620 'North Borneo'	45641 'Sandwich'	ex Burton M.P.D.

```
TUESDAY AND WEDNESDAY, 17TH AND 18TH MARCH.   ...

8X76 - 9.15am Staveley M.P.D. to Crewe Works.

Horns Bridge        GL  pass 10X31am    Derby North Jn.        arr 12L20pm
Clay Cross North Jn.    arr  10*42        -do-            GL  dep 12L22
   -do-         ML  dep  11* 9        London Road Jn.        pass 12.28
Clay Cross South Jn.    pass 11.12       L.N.W. Jn.         ML  pass 12X33
Stretton            pass 11.18       Melbourne Jn.          pass 12.36
Ambergate       AL  pass 11.40        Stenson Jn.            pass 12.50
Ambergate South Jn. GL  pass 11X42        Egginton Jn.           pass  1. 4
Broadholme      ML  pass 11X54        Marston Jn.            pass  1. 8
                            Tutbury            pass  1.12

Tuesday :   Steam Hauled "dead" 45683 and 45536
Wednesday :    "       "      "  45725 and 45576

MAXIMUM SPEED 25 m.p.h.

Permission has been given by the Chief Civil Engineer for these trains to travel
    over the timed route in accordance with the General Appendix Instructions, pages
    97 and 98.

"Rider" to travel on "dead" engine.

Eastern Region (Barrow Hill) P.  Class 8F throughout and LE to Derby M.P.D.
    Enginemen to Derby North Jn.  Home as required.
Derby M.P.D.  Arrange enginemen Derby North Jn. to Crewe Works.  Return LE or as
    required.


MONDAY, 16TH NOVEMBER. 19..

8Z82 - Trafford Park M.P.D. to Great Bridge (J.Cashmore Ltd.)

Millers Dale            pass 12 16  Melbourne Jn.         pass 14 39
Rowsley Station         arr  12L45  Stenson Jn.           pass 14 48
   -do-            dep  12W50  Repton & Willington       pass 14 52
Ambergate           pass 13 20  Burton            pass 15 05
Ambergate South Jn. SL  pass 13X22  Leicester Jn.      GL  pass 15XO7
Broadholme          arr  13*30  Branston Jn.          arr  15W12
   -do-         ML  dep  14*04    -do-            dep  15W18
Derby North Jn.     GL  pass 14X27  Dunstall          ML  pass 15X27
London Road Jn.         pass 14 32  Wichnor Jn.           pass 15 36
L.N.W. Jn.          ML  pass 14 37  Lichfield TV (HL)         pass 15 54

Conveys one "dead" engine Class 6P No.45579 (with rider)

MAXIMUM SPEED 25 M.P.H.

M.W.Line (Trafford Park) P.  through.  Enginemen and Rider to Rowsley.
    Return as required.
Rowsley Enginemen and Rider Rowsley to Branston Jn.  Return as required.
Burton Enginemen and Rider Branston Junction to Great Bridge.  Return
    LE or as required.
```

```
8X96 - 46122, 46156 Class 7P 4-6-0 Engines hauled 'Dead' to Dairycoates, Hull
    (A. Draper & Son, No. 7 Section).

Annesley M.P.D.         dep  11 25  Kirkby South Jn.      pass 11 34
Annesley North Jn.      pass 11 30  Pilsley           pass 11 52
```

MAXIMUM SPEED 25 M.P.H.

Marshalled:- Hauling engine, two runner wagons, dead engine, two runner wagons,
dead engine and brakevan.

Annesley P. (Class 5) throughout, and Enginemen to Mexborough No.1, return as required
Annesley G. to Mexborough.   Home as required.

Permission has been given by the Chief Civil Engineer for this train to travel over th
timed route.

THE INSTRUCTIONS SHOWN ON PAGES 97 TO 98 OF THE GENERAL APPENDIX MUST BE OBSERVED BY
ALL CONCERNED.   **-1 JAN 1965**

-2-

NO. 1567 (Continued)

FRIDAY, 1ST JANUARY, 1965

8X97 - To Risca (Messrs. Bird (Swansea) Ltd., Pontymister Works).

Annesley Yard		dep	10 30	Long Eaton Jn		pass	12 33
Annesley South Jn		pass	10 35	Trent		pass	12 37
Bulwell Common		pass	10 48	Sheet Stores Jn		pass	12 40
Bagthorpe Jn		pass	10 51	Lock Lane Crossing		pass	12 44
Nottingham Vic.		pass	11 00	Chellaston Jn		pass	13 07
Trent Lane Jn		arr	11*10	Stenson Jn		arr	13*20
-do-) PRO-		dep	11*22	-do-		dep	13*44
Exchange Sdgs) PEL		arr	11L27	Repton & Willington		pass	13 49
		RUN ROUND		Clay Mills Jn	GL	pass	13X56
-do-		dep	11L45	Leicester Jn		pass	14 12
Sneinton Jn		arr	11*50	Branston Jn		arr	14W17
-do-	GL	dep	11*54	-do-		dep	14W23
London Road Jn		pass	11 59	Dunstall	ML	pass	14X33
Wilford Road		arr	12W04	Wichnor Jn		pass	14 42
-do-		dep	12W10	Alrewas		pass	14 48
Mansfield Jn	LL	pass	12X15	Lichfield T.V. (H.L.)		pass	15 05
Beeston North Jn		pass	12 20				

Conveys condemned Class 7P 4-6-0 Engine No.46163 hauled 'dead' (with rider)

MAXIMUM SPEED 25 M.P.H.

Annesley P. (Class 5) to Stourbridge, and enginemen to Exchange Sidings, relief by
NNM men, and home as required.
Nottingham M.P.D. arrange enginemen relieve ANN men Exchange Sidings at 11 27, work
to Branston Jn. 14 17, relief by BUT men, and home as required.
Burton M.P.D. arrange enginemen relieve NNM men Branston Jn. 14 17, work to
Stourbridge and home with engine or as required.

8Z91 - To Great Bridge (J. Cashmore Ltd.) **20 NOV 1964**

Nottingham M.P.D.		dep	05 16	Stenson Jn.		dep	06*30
Mansfield Jn.	ML	dep	05*20	Repton & W.		pass	06 35
Trent		pass	05 38	Burton		pass	06 51
Sheet Stores Jn.		pass	05 41	Leicester Jn.		pass	06 53
Lock Lane Crossing		pass	05 45	Wichnor Jn.		pass	07 06
Chellaston Jn.		pass	06 08	Alrewas		pass	07 11
Stenson Jn.		arr	06*21	Lichfield T.V. (H.L.)		pass	07 24

Conveys one "dead" locomotive (Class 6P No. 45564) (with rider).

MAXIMUM SPEED 25 M.P.H.

Nottingham P. return as required.

8Z97 - To Great Bridge (J. Cashmore Ltd.) **20 NOV 1964**

Saltley M.P.D.	GL	dep	09 15	Sutton Park	pass 09 45
Washwood Heath Jn.		pass	09 21	Aldridge Jn.	pass 09 59
Castle Bromwich Jn.		pass	09 27	Lichfield Road Jn.	pass 10 05
Park Lane Jn.		pass	09 32		

Conveys "dead" locomotive Nos. 45631 (Class 6P 4-6-0), 44516 and 44226 (Class 4F 0-6-0).

"Riders" to travel on last two "dead" locomotives.

Saltley P. return L or as required.

FRIDAY, 4TH DECEMBER. 1964

8Z28 - To Great Bridge (J.Cashmore Ltd.)

Derby M.P.D.		dep	09 05	Repton & W.	pass	09 35
E.S.S. No. 1		arr	09*09	Burton	pass	09 49
-do-		dep	09*11	Leicester Jn.	pass	09 51
London Road Jn.		pass	09 15	Wichnor Jn.	pass	10 04
L.N.W. Jn.	ML	pass	09X20	Alrewas	pass	10 10
Melbourne Jn.		pass	09 22	Lichfield T.V. (H.L.)	pass	10 24
Stenson Jn.		pass	09 30			

Conveys "Condemned" Locomotives Nos. 45561, 45622, 45611 and 45557 (Ex LMS Class 6P
4-6-0s)

"Riders" to travel on second and last "dead" engines.

MAXIMUM SPEED 25 M.P.H.

Derby P. - Return L or as required.

_____

MONDAY, 4TH JANUARY. 1965

8Z29 - To Great Bridge (J. Cashmore's Sidings). (Conveys "Condemned" Locomotives
Nos. 44332 and 44552 (Class 4F 0-6-0), 45620 and 45641 (Class 6P 4-6-0).)

Burton M.P.D.	dep	10 30	Wichnor Jn.	pass	10 50
Leicester Jn.	arr	10*33	Alrewas	pass	10 55
-do-	dep	10*35	Lichfield T.V. (H.L.)	pass	11 11

"Rider" to travel on second and rear "dead" locomotives.

MAXIMUM SPEED 25 M.P.H.

Burton M.P.D. P. Return L.E. or as required.

8X96 - 46122, 46156 Class 7P 4-6-0 Engines hauled 'Dead' to Dairycoates, Hull
(A. Draper & Son, No. 7 Section).

Annesley M.P.D.	dep	11 25	Kirkby South Jn.	pass	11 34
Annesley North Jn.	pass	11 30	Pilsley	pass	11 52

MAXIMUM SPEED 25 M.P.H.

Marshalled:- Hauling engine, two runner wagons, dead engine, two runner wagons,
dead engine and brakevan.

Annesley P. (Class 5) throughout, and Enginemen to Mexborough No.1, return as required
Annesley G. to Mexborough. Home as required.

Permission has been given by the Chief Civil Engineer for this train to travel over th
timed route.

THE INSTRUCTIONS SHOWN ON PAGES 97 TO 98 OF THE GENERAL APPENDIX MUST BE OBSERVED BY
ALL CONCERNED.   -1 JAN 1965

-2-

NO. 1567 (Continued)

FRIDAY, 1ST JANUARY. 1965

8X97 - To Risca (Messrs. Bird (Swansea) Ltd., Pontymister Works).

Annesley Yard		dep	10 30	Long Eaton Jn	pass	12 33
Annesley South Jn		pass	10 35	Trent	pass	12 37
Bulwell Common		pass	10 48	Sheet Stores Jn	pass	12 40
Bagthorpe Jn		pass	10 51	Lock Lane Crossing	pass	12 44
Nottingham Vic.		pass	11 00	Chellaston Jn	pass	13 07
Trent Lane Jn		arr	11*10	Stenson Jn	arr	13*20
-do-) PRO-		dep	11*22	-do-	dep	13*44
Exchange Sdgs) PEL		arr	11L27	Repton & Willington	pass	13 49
		RUN ROUND		Clay Mills Jn	GL pass	13X56
-do-		dep	11L45	Leicester Jn	pass	14 12
Sneinton Jn		arr	11*50	Branston Jn	arr	14W17
-do-	GL	dep	11*54	-do-	dep	14W23
London Road Jn		pass	11 59	Dunstall	ML pass	14X33
Wilford Road		arr	12W04	Wichnor Jn	pass	14 42
-do-		dep	12W10	Alrewas	pass	14 48
Mansfield Jn	LL	pass	12X15	Lichfield T.V. (H.L.)	pass	15 05
Beeston North Jn		pass	12 20			

```
Conveys condemned Class 7P 4-6-0 Engine No.46163 hauled 'dead' (with rider)

MAXIMUM SPEED 25 M.P.H.

Annesley P. (Class 5)  to Stourbridge, and enginemen to Exchange Sidings, relief by
    NNM men, and home as required.
Nottingham M.P.D. arrange enginemen relieve ANN men Exchange Sidings at 11 27, work
    to Branston Jn. 14 17, relief by BAT men, and home as required.
Burton M.P.D. arrange enginemen relieve NNM men Branston Jn. 14 17, work to
    Stourbridge and home with engine or as required.
```

* * *

The weather was befitting of the occasion when rebuilt 'Jubilee' No. 45735 'Comet' and 'Royal Scot' No. 46125 '3rd Carabinier' were hauled through Trent station on 13th January 1965 en-route from Annesley to Great Bridge. Earlier, in September another 'Royal Scot' No. 46112 'Sherwood Forester' was despatched from Annesley, on that occasion running via the ex-GN route through Derby Friargate – this line having lost its passenger services a couple of weeks earlier – to Eggington Junction. Indeed, Annesley was having a clearout of its ex-LMS locomotives, for on 1st January 'Royal Scots' Nos. 46122 'Royal Ulster Rifleman' and 46156 'The South Wales Borderer' were hauled to Dairycoates, Hull for A. Draper & Son, No. 7 Section. This move ran as a train with two runner wagons between the condemned engines with a brakevan at the rear. Also on New Years Day (postponed from 17th December) 'Royal Scot' No. 46163 'Civil Service Rifleman' was arranged to go to Pontyminster Works, Risca for Messrs Bird Ltd; and for a second time the move was cancelled, the stay of execution lasting until 5th March. A further movement this time to Beighton for Messrs T.W.Ward Ltd. took place on 1st February when Royal Scot No. 46165 'The Ranger (12th London Regt.)' was hauled to its final resting place.

* * *

All locations concerned with the movement of trains were issued with working timetables, passenger and freight, together with the associated sectional and general appendix to the working time table and books of rules and regulations, also supplementary notices. There was also the weekly engineering notice and a weekly train notice that contained altered and additional workings, in addition Special Notices were issued by the Trains Office at Derby. These included all manner of movements from test trains to locomotives going to the breakers yard.

Each notice was numbered and appended: The following to acknowledge receipt of this Notice by telegram to "Trains NP, Derby" using the code "ARNO S.N. XXX":

M.P.D. – Whichever depot was involved in the workings.
D.M. – Divisional Manager. D.C. – District Control Office.
Y.M. – Yard Masters Office. S.M. – Station Master.

* * *

The station foreman at Trent was responsible for sorting the notices and arranging their distribution to the local signal boxes. Few options were available in getting them to outlying locations, the lamp man being utilised occasionally, on Fridays (pay day) they were given to the respective signalmen. Most however were given to the guard of a passenger train to throw them out when passing the signal boxes which would have been advised of their expectance in advance. At Trent Junction the train would not have been going too fast, no problem at Sheet Stores with the permanent speed restriction over the junction. Ratcliffe Junction signal box however was a different kettle of fish as the train would now be well into its stride. Trains passing on the down and up goods lines often hindered this delivery; it was not unknown for the notices to land in a coal wagon bound for Brent yard. The prevailing wind with none too good an aim from the guard would result in recovery from an adjacent cornfield.

*   *   *

On Sunday 24th January, perhaps the greatest wartime leader, certainly this century, Sir Winston Churchill died. The following Thursday, being my rest day I journeyed to Westminster for the lying in state. It was a bitterly cold day with snow showers; the queue to view was considerable. The State Funeral took place on the Saturday, S.R. Pacific No. 34051 'Sir Winston Churchill' being turned out to haul the special train from Waterloo to Han(d)borough station with internment in Bladen churchyard.

1965 was the beginning of the rationalisation of Summer Seasonal Services on the Great Central line, which was about to be truncated before complete closure. Also in 1965 I had two interviews for clerical posts in the Line Managers Office at Derby, the first in the Passenger Rolling Stock section and the other in the Freight section, neither of which was I successful. Forrester Fielding an ex- military fellow with a bristling moustache took the interview for the PRS position. During the meeting I made reference to Pat Egan, Chief Investigator for the NE/SW services in the LMO in Derby. Fielding admonished me for the familiarity towards one of his inspectors, and from that point the interview went downhill. What probably made matter worse was to refer to him as Pat, his name being Wilf. He lived in Long Eaton and travelled to Derby frequently from Trent and we would often converse whilst he waited for his train. Speaking to him later I reflected on the interview, he wasn't at all concerned what Fielding had to say. If there was one position I coveted it was that of Chief Investigator NE/SW.

After a few months of having various relief stationmasters at Trent, Bert Callard appeared on the scene from Kirkby. It was quite amusing to see him trying to manoeuvre himself in the company of Jim Barnes the District Signalman's Inspector in an effort to procure a Sunday turn in connection with engineering work. Jim however appeared to keep the socialising at a distance. Soon Bert became obsessed over what he deduced was my manipulation of free tickets; he was convinced that there was some misuse of them, but he could not figure out the way that they were being used. It was simplistic; the majority of the tickets were made out from Bournemouth (although on one occasion it was from the French Ports) to Aberdeen. The dating of each free ticket was crucial, I needed to use the return part (the journey to Aberdeen being undertaken earlier) to go to the south-coast and then to use the new ticket and repeat the process.

Each time Bert handed me my free pass he reiterated that it was only a matter of time before I would get caught. Imagine his sheer delight when he sent me a letter stating, 'The Divisional Manager, Nottingham has called for an explanation of your use of Free Ticket No. 8785'. He retorted, "I knew you would get caught, I warned you". There was a hint of gratification in the tone of his voice. I submitted a report outlining the journeys and the routes taken, it also contained cosmetic information, which was included facetiously. Not wishing to declare all to Bert Callard, no mention was made of the journey to Southampton, which was undertaken of course using the previous ticket.

"Free Ticket No. 8785. Bournemouth to Aberdeen. Tuesday 23rd February 1965, I joined the 10.50 a.m. Bournemouth-York at Southampton, departed six minutes late,

BRITISH RAILWAYS BOARD
LONDON MIDLAND REGION.

To : Station Master
..........Trent...............

From : Divisional Manager's Office,
         NOTTINGHAM
Ref   : P3/Summer/1965.
Extn : 41
Date : 10th December, 1964.

SUMMER SEASONAL SERVICES - SUMMER 1965.

I give below details of the services which it is proposed to run in the timetable commencing Monday, 14th June, 1965.

It must be borne in mind of course, that this information is given only as a guide and firm timings must NOT be quoted, until this information is confirmed. Full details of timings etc, will be circulated at a later date.

TRAIN	OPERATIVE DATES
8.25am (SO) Leicester London Rd. to Blackpool to depart 8.0am to connect into 8.25am Nottingham Midland to Llandudno at Derby Midland.	26th June to 11th September.
7.22am (SO) Nottingham Midland to Blackpool	17th July to 28th August
8.30am Newcastle to Bournemouth to continue via G.C.	14th June to 4th September
9.45pm (FO) Leeds to Bournemouth W.. to run via the Erewash Valley calling at Nottingham Midland and reverse.	))) 16th July to 13th August))
to start from Nottingham Midland calling at Loughborough Midland and Leicester London Rd thence via Kelmarsh	)) 2nd and 9th July))
7.35am (SO) Nottingham Midland to Bournemouth	to be cancelled.
9. 0am (SO) Sheffield Victoria to Bournemouth to start from Sheffield Midland calling at Derby Midland and Birmingham New St. thence via Barnt Green and Oxford.	19th June to 4th September
6.15am (SO) Derby Midland to Bristol T.M. to be extended to Weymouth	19th June to 4th September.
7.35am (SO) Sheffield Midland to Bristol T.M. to be extended to Paignton	19th June to 4th September.
8.40am (SUN) Sheffield Midland to Bristol T.M. to start back at Bradford F.S. and extended to Penzance.	14th June 1965 to 12th June 1966.
10.25pm (FO) Manchester Piccadilly to Eastbourne to run via the Erewash Valley to Nottingham Midland (reverse) calling at Loughborough Midland and Leicester Ldn Rd. Thence via Brent Jcn and Acton Wells.	16th July to 13th August

Continued.............

TRAIN	OPERATIVE DATES
7.58am (SO) Nottingham Midland to Llandudno to be retimed to depart 8.25am and call at Beeston, Sawley Jcn, Draycott, Borrowash, Spondon and Derby Midland.	19th June to 4th September.
8.35am (SO) Nottingham Victoria to Mablethorpe to start from Nottingham Midland at 8.30am thence via Netherfield Jcn	3rd July to 28th August
9.50am (SO) Leicester Central to Mablethorpe to start from Leicester London Rd calling at Loughborough Midland and Nottingham Midland thence via Netherfield Jcn.	19th June to 11th September
8.10am (SO) Derby Friargate to Mablethorpe to start from Derby Midland at 8.30am calling at Sawley Jcn and Nottingham Midland, thence via Netherfield Jcn.	19th June to 11th September
9.20am (SX) Nottingham Victoria to Mablethorpe to start from Nottingham Midland thence via Netherfield Jcn.	26th July to 3rd September.
9.50am (SUN) Basford North to Mablethorpe to start from Derby Midland at 9.30am calling at Sawley Jcn, and Nottingham Midland, thence via Netherfield Jcn.	18th July to 29th August
8.45pm (FO) Bradford F.S. to Newton Abbot to be extended to Paignton.	18th June to 3rd September.
7.30pm (FO) Sheffield Midland to Newquay to start from Nottingham Midland approx. 8.45pm calling at Sawley Jcn, Derby Midland, Tamworth and Birmingham New St.	18th June to 3rd September
9.48pm (FO) Nottingham Midland to Paignton	2nd July to 27th August.
10.05pm (FO) Hull to Paignton	18th June to 3rd September.
10.13pm (FO) Sheffield Midland to Paignton	to be cancelled.
9.05pm (FO) Newcastle to Paignton	18th June to 6th August.
7.30am (SO) Newcastle to Paignton to call additionally at Birmingham New St.	19th June to 4th September
8.52am (SO) Sheffield Midland to Paignton	19th June to 4th September
9.05am (SO) Bradford F.S. to Paignton to run to Plymouth.	10th July to 28th August
8.10am (SO) Sheffield Midland to Penzance NOT to convey Paignton portion To start from Bradford F.S. at 7.05am as booked for S.X.	19th June to 4th September
7.20pm (FO) Sheffield Midland to Penzance	18th June to 3rd September.

Continued........

- 3 -

TRAIN	OPERATIVE DATES

7.43am (SO) Nottingham Midland to Plymouth
    to depart Nottingham approx. 7.55am
    calling additionally at Spondon and
    terminating at Bristol T.M.

19th June to 4th
    September

10.05pm (FO) Sheffield Victoria to Portsmouth
    to run via the Erewash Valley calling
    at Nottingham Midland (reverse) Loughborough
    Midland and Leicester London Rd., thence via
    Nuneaton and Barnt Green.

18th June to 3rd
    September

9.55am (SO) Leeds to Poole
    to run via the Erewash Valley calling at
    Loughborough Midland and Leicester London Rd
    thence via Kelmarsh.

19th June to 4th
    September

11.35pm (FO) Derby Friargate to Ramsgate
    to start from Nottingham Midland calling
    at Trent, Loughborough Midland and Leicester
    London Rd (10.20pm Derby Mid - Nottingham
    to connect) thence via Brent and Acton Wells.

2nd July to 13th August

8.10am (SO) Leicester London Rd to Scarborough
    to depart 7.50am and run via and call at
    Beeston and Nottingham Midland
    (reverse) thence via Trowell NON-STOP to
    Chesterfield.

3rd July to 28th August

8.23am (SO) Kings Norton to Scarborough
    to run via Filey H.C.

19th June to 4th September

8.30am (SO) Nottingham Midland to Scarborough

to be cancelled.

9.30am (SO) Derby Midland to Cromer & Sheringham
    to combine at Luffenham with
    9.55am from Leicester London Rd.

3rd July to 28th August

8.55am (SO) Derby Friargate to Skegness
    to start from Derby Midland calling at
    Sawley Jcn and Nottingham Midland
    thence via Netherfield Jcn.

19th June to 11th
    September

6.38am (SO) Radford to Skegness/Mablethorpe

to be cancelled.

8.50am (SO) Kings Norton to Skegness
    to run via and call additionally
    at Derby Midland thence via Netherfield Jcn

10th July to 28th August

8.05am (SO) Nottingham Victoria to Skegness
    to start from Nottingham Midland
    thence via Netherfield Jcn.

3rd July to 4th
    September

9.50am (SO) Derby Friargate to Skegness

to be cancelled.

9.15am (SUN) Basford North to Skegness
    to start from Derby Midland
    at 9.0am calling at Sawley Jcn
    and Nottingham Midland thence via
    Netherfield Jcn.

27th June to 5th
    September

9.20am (SO) Leicester Central to Skegness
    to start from Leicester London Rd.
    calling at Loughborough Mid
    and Nottingham Midland thence
    via Netherfield Jcn.

19th June to 11th
    September

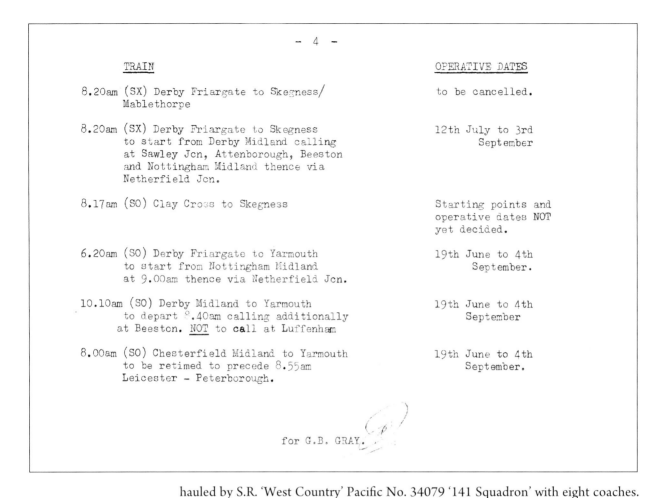

- 4 -

TRAIN	OPERATIVE DATES
8.20am (SX) Derby Friargate to Skegness/ Mablethorpe	to be cancelled.
8.20am (SX) Derby Friargate to Skegness to start from Derby Midland calling at Sawley Jcn, Attenborough, Beeston and Nottingham Midland thence via Netherfield Jcn.	12th July to 3rd September
8.17am (SO) Clay Cross to Skegness	Starting points and operative dates NOT yet decided.
6.20am (SO) Derby Friargate to Yarmouth to start from Nottingham Midland at 9.00am thence via Netherfield Jcn.	19th June to 4th September.
10.10am (SO) Derby Midland to Yarmouth to depart 9.40am calling additionally at Beeston. NOT to call at Luffenham	19th June to 4th September
8.00am (SO) Chesterfield Midland to Yarmouth to be retimed to precede 8.55am Leicester - Peterborough.	19th June to 4th September.

for G.B. GRAY.

hauled by S.R. 'West Country' Pacific No. 34079 '141 Squadron' with eight coaches. Despite being brought to a stand outside Reading West, the train arrived at Oxford on time, there, No. 34079 was replaced by W.R. 'Hall' No. 5933 'Kingswy Hall' departing two minutes late. A further rostered engine change took place at Banbury where the steam locomotive was replaced by English Electric Type '3' diesel No. D6797 for the final leg to York. The train arrived at Nottingham Victoria four minutes early at 4.32 p.m. where I alighted, this being a legitimate break of journey which would be resumed almost three weeks later. As I passed through the ticket barrier the ticket collector punched my ticket. Resuming my journey northwards on Monday 15th March, my ticket was once

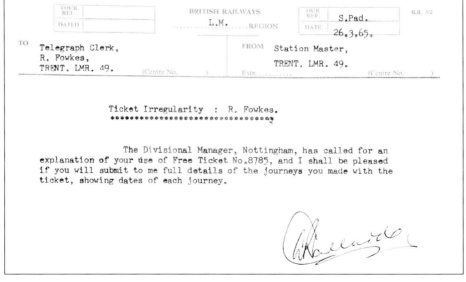

YOUR REF		BRITISH RAILWAYS	OUR REF	S.Pad.	B.R. 3/2
DATED		L.M. ....REGION	DATE	26.3.65.	

TO   Telegraph Clerk,   FROM   Station Master,
      R. Fowkes,
      TRENT. LMR. 49.   (Centre No.   )   Extn. ....   TRENT. LMR. 49.   (Centre No.   )

Ticket Irregularity : R. Fowkes.
****

        The Divisional Manager, Nottingham, has called for an explanation of your use of Free Ticket No. 8785, and I shall be pleased if you will submit to me full details of the journeys you made with the ticket, showing dates of each journey.

again clipped at the Nottingham Victoria ticket barrier before catching the 8.25 p.m. DMU to Grantham. There I joined the 'Aberdonian' hauled by its customary English Electric 'Deltic' diesel No. D9004 'Queen's Own Highlander' as far as Edinburgh where an E. E. Type '4' diesel took over for the final stage to Aberdeen. With an arrival time of 6.38 a.m., there was just time for a cup of coffee before boarding the 7.10 a.m. 'Bon Accord' to Glasgow Buchanan Street with Gresley A4 Pacific No. 60009 'Union of South Africa' at the head of a six coach train. The gradient of 1 in 96 to Ferryhill Junction with five miles of unbroken climbing past Cove Bay was a gruelling start for a 'cold' engine albeit with only a 200-ton load, No. 60009 almost stalling between the station and Ferryhill Junction. The train was three minutes late from Stonehaven, six late from Forfar owing to a permanent way slack and four minutes late departing Perth. A dead stand on leaving there put the train ten minutes late leaving Stirling and arrived in Glasgow at 10.18 a.m. – Eight minutes late. Some of those arrears would have been recovered but for a further permanent way check and signal checks at Dunblane and Bridge of Allan. It was in the vicinity of Stirling that a Travelling Ticket Inspector examined my free pass. He informed me that the ticket was being retained as it had two cancel holes in it. The TTC issued me with free excess endorsed – ticket held for investigation. Subsequent examination of the paper ticket raised a few eyebrows". On my next turn of duty I presented the report to Bert Callard, who, after reading it expressed his concern regarding the content, of which I said I was not prepared to amend. In addition to handing him the report, just for good measure, I also submitted an application for a further free ticket from Weymouth to Aberdeen. Needless to say nothing more was heard regarding the 'alleged' ticket irregularity. The two-cancel holes were in fact done at Nottingham Victoria station.

* * *

The Locomotive Club of Great Britain ran a steam hauled Parspec from St. Pancras to Skegness and return on 24th April 1965. Motive power from London to Nottingham and back was with 'Britannia' Pacific No. 70052 'Firth of Tay'. Eastern Region 'B1' No. 61406 worked the train forward to Skegness and return, with Class '4F' No. 44401 providing assistance from Nottingham to Shirebrook West. With Nottingham motive power depot in the throws of closure 70052 ran light to Toton for servicing prior to its return working. Toton enginemen were booked to work the return leg back to St. Pancras, apart from short notice diversions and the occasional 'attached' working, the depot had no rostered passenger work. Driver William (Bill) Webb was entrusted with 70052 on the LCGB special from Nottingham to London. He told me some years later that he was unaware until signing on duty on the Saturday afternoon that he was working an express. In the lobby he told his fireman, "C'mon Jack we're going to London"; "on a diesel" was the reply, "no with a steamer" said Bill, "oh blimey" Jack uttered. Having been down to Trent Junction earlier that morning to photograph the LCGB Special and then again to Toton where the loco was being serviced, I was late turn telegraph clerk at Trent on that particular day. Spoke to the shed foreman at the depot, to ask the driver if he would oblige with a chime when passing North Erewash Junction and Long Eaton Junction signal boxes on its way to Nottingham. The signalmen at the two boxes were alerted to this and had the telephone receiver off the hook as 'Firth of Tay' went by. The LCGB special had arrived on time from Skegness, but was a minute late leaving Nottingham and six minutes late passing Melton Junction, a combination of a cold-engine and a permanent way check at Edwalton, the arrears being recouped by Kettering. During the scheduled stop at Wellingborough for water, the train organiser came up to the engine and said to the driver that if a punctual arrival at St. Pancras was realised then there would be something in it for them. Although Bill signed for both the main and goods lines, it was usual for freight trains to use the goods lines between Wellingborough and Sharnbrook, as this was an easier gradient than the main line. The Locomotive Inspector probably had this in mind when he suggested that on leaving Wellingborough, 70052 be given some regulator. The approach into St. Pancras was funereally slow, Bill wanting to avoid at all cost coming into contact with the buffer stops, so slow in fact, that enthusiasts were alighting onto the platform from the train and walking alongside the engine. The arrival was on time and the organiser handed the driver five crisp ten-shilling notes in numbered sequence. Bill regaled many over the years with this tale, adding – "not bad for a freight train driver"!

(PRIVATE and not for publication)   B.R. 358/5

LONDON MIDLAND REGION
(Midland Lines)

S P E C I A L   N O T I C E   NO.406

SATURDAY, 24TH APRIL 1965

1X28 – Parspec to Skegness.   V. Special Limit. (Locomotive Club of Great Britain)

Cricklewood C.S.	UL	dep	07/30	Shirebrook West	arr	11L55
West Hampstead	GL	pass	07X38	–do–	dep	11L57
St.Pancras		arr	07/58		Via Eastern Region	
–do–		dep	08 25	Netherfield & C.	pass	17 57
Finchley Road		pass	08 32½	Nottingham Mid.	arr	18L05
Hendon		pass	08 37	–do–	dep	18L12
St.Albans		pass	08 50		(1)	
Luton		pass	08 59½	Widmerpool	pass	18 26
Bedford North		arr	09W21	Melton Jn.	pass	18 35
–do–		dep	09W27	Oakham	pass	18 48
Sharnbrook Summit		pass	09 40	Manton	pass	18 52
			(4)	Corby	pass	19 02
Wellingborough		pass	09 48½		(2)	
Kettering	3	pass	09 55	Glendon South	SL	pass	19 08½
Desborough North		pass	10 02½	Kettering	pass	19 12½
Market Harborough		pass	10 08	Kettering Jn.	ML	pass	19X15½
Kibworth North		pass	10 16	Wellingborough	arr	19 23
Wigston North Jn.		pass	10 24	–do–	dep	19W30
Leicester		arr	10 30	Sharnbrook Summit	pass	19 39
do		dep	10W36		(2)	
Syston		pass	10 42	Bedford	pass	19 50
Loughborough		pass	10 49	Flitwick	pass	19 59
Trent		pass	11 00	Luton	pass	20 09
Nottingham Mid.		arr	11L10	St.Albans	pass	20 18
–do–		dep	11L22		(4)	
Mansfield Jn.		pass	11 24	Hendon	pass	20 32
Basford V.		pass	11 30	Finchley Road	pass	20 35
Hucknall B.		pass	11 35	St.Pancras	arr	20 40
Newstead		pass	11 38	–do–	GL	dep	20/55
Kirkby		pass	11 43	West Hampstead	FL	pass	21X14
Mansfield T.		pass	11 49	Watling St.	LL	pass	21X19
				Cricklewood C.S.	arr	21/24

15 40 Lawley Street to Neilsons Sidings 4F08 follow from Kettering Jn.

0X28 – L.E. from Willesden M.P.D.				0W00 – L.E. to Willesden M.P.D.			
Acton Canal Wharf		arr	07*02	St.Pancras	GL	dep	20/58
–do–		dep	07*05	Carlton Road Jn.		pass	21 10
Dudding Hill Jn.		pass	07 15	Cricklewood Jn.		pass	21 28
Cricklewood Jn.	GL	pass	07 20	Dudding Hill Jn.		pass	21 33
Carlton Road Jn.		pass	07 35	Acton Canal Wharf		arr	21*43
St.Pancras		arr	07/45	–do–		dep	21*46

L.E. to work from Nottingham to Skegness and return portion of journey. Colwick M.P.D.
    depart 10/32, Netherfield & C. pass 10 42, Nottingham Mid. arrive 10/50.
    Rep. No.0X28.

0X 28 – L.E. (To assist 1X28 Nottingham to Shirebrook West)

Kirkby M.P.D.	dep	10/15	Mansfield Jn.	pass	10 48
Hucknall	pass	10 29	Nottingham Mid.	arr	10/50
Bulwell	pass	10 36			

0X28 – (After working 1X28)

Nottingham Mid.	dep	11/35	North Erewash Jn.	pass	11 54
Long Eaton Jn.	pass	11 50	Toton M.P.D.	arr	12/04

Bill – Maureen's uncle – was himself no stranger to the Britannia Pacific locomotive as he had worked many years earlier the double-headed fully-fitted Toton-Brent coal trials. The Flying Collier with 70020 'Mercury' and 70023 'Venus' were the engines involved, hauling 70 x -16ton loaded wagons with a dynamometer car and on arrival at Brent was featured in the 1952 March edition of Coal magazine.

```
            B R I T I S H   R A I L W A Y S.        ERO. 46108.
            LONDON MIDLAND OPERATING AREA.
                    (Midland Division).
               S P E C I A L   N O T I C E.         No. 62.
    This Notice must be kept strictly private and not given to the public.
    SUNDAY, JANUARY 20TH.
    Special Test - Class C. (conveys 70 loaded 16 ton wagons (Vacuum Fitted)
    (Modified Class "C" Running Times).
    Toton Sidings  HL   dep.   9.33am   Wellingboro'          dep.   11E32am
    Ratcliffe Jc.  PL   pass   9.43     (Finedon Rd)
    Hathern             pass   9.49     Irchester South       pass   11.44
    Loughboro'          pass   9.52     Souldrop              pass   11.55
    Syston North Jc.    pass  10. 3     Oakley Stn.           pass   12. 1pm
    Melton              pass  10.20     Bedford               pass   12. 4
    Manton              pass  10.41     Leagrave     )GL      pass   12.33
    Wing Sds.           pass  10.43     Luton        ) &      pass   12.36
    Glendon Sth.Jc.SL   pass  11. 3     Harpenden Jc.)SL      pass   12.42
    Kettering           pass  11. 7     St.Albans    )        pass   12.49
    Kettering Jc.FL     pass  11. 9     Radlett               pass   12.54
    Wellingboro'        arr.  11W17     Hendon                pass    1. 4
    (Finedon Rd)                        Brent Sth. Sds.       arr.    1.11

    TOTON P. Two B.R. Class 7 (4.6.2) engines.
    TOTON enginemen throughout and home passenger.
    TOTON G. throughout and home passenger.

    To be marshalled :- Engines, Dynamometer Car, 70 loaded 16-ton mineral
                        wagons, 20 ton fitted brakevan.
                        SPECIAL INSTRUCTIONS.
    (1) The Special train will be signalled by the Special IS LINE CLEAR
        signal 3-4-2.

    (2) Except as shown in paragraph (4) below, permission must not be given
        for the Special train to approach from the Signal Box in the rear
        until the "TRAINS OUT OF SECTION" signal has been received from the
        Signal Box in advance for the previous train passing over the line
        upon which the Special train will run, and the block indicator
        (where provided), worked from that box, is in the normal position.

    (3) The Signalman at a Signal Box where the outermost Home Signal is
        less than half-a-mile from the outermost Home signal of the box in
        advance must not give permission for the Special Train to approach
        from the Signal Box in the rear until permission has been obtained
        for it to proceed to the Signal Box in advance.
    (4) Permission must not be given for the Special train to approach from
        the Signalbox in rear at a Signal Box where there is an intermediate
        Block Home Signal worked from the Signal Box in rear until the line
        is clear up to and including the overlap circuit of the intermediate
        Block Home Signal.
    (5) The Special Train must not be allowed to proceed towards an inter-
        mediate Block Home Signal worked from the Signal Box in rear until
        the "TRAINS OUT OF SECTION" signal has been received from the Signal
        Box in advance for the previous train and the block indicator (where
        provided), worked from the box is in the normal position.
    The following to acknowledge immediately on receipt of this Notice by
    telegram to "Trains N.P. Derby" using the code "A.NO. S.N. 62":-
    M.P. Depots - Toton,
```

What rankled Bill, was that Stan Woods, the junior driver on the leading engine 'Mercury' was interviewed and photographed whilst he didn't even get a mention. Other high speed trials of coal trains to Brent were not without incident, Bill recalled on another of his turns, also with a brace of Britannias, that by the time Wellingborough was reached, there were no fewer than nine hot axle boxes on the train which had to be detached, which was time consuming as the train was fully wired up throughout. Bill was involved

Driver William Webb (left)
and fireman Eric Sims working
on the *Flying Collier*.

William Webb.

```
        B R I T I S H   R A I L W A Y S        LRO. 46108.
        LONDON MIDLAND OPERATING AREA
        (Midland Division)

        S P E C I A L   N O T I C E           NO. 1732.
This Notice must be kept strictly private and not given to the public.

SUNDAY, 7TH DECEMBER.

Special Test - Class 'C'.  Conveys Brake Test Unit. 52 empty 16-ton
                wagons.(Vacuum Fitted - screw coupled).

Toton Sidings  )G    dep.  9.20am   Bedford Jcn.   )SL     dep. 12.55p
Long Eaton Sta.)L    pass  9.26     Oakley Sta.    ) &     pass  1. 3
Trent          )     pass  9.30     Souldrop       )GL     pass  1.14
Ratcliffe Jcn. )     pass  9.34     Irchester South)       pass  1.22
Hathern        )G    pass  9.41     Wellingboro'           pass  1.27
Loughboro'     )L    pass  9.46     Kettering              pass  1.39
Sileby         )     pass  9.55     Glendon South Jcn.     pass  1.43
Syston North Jcn.    pass 10. 0     Desboro' North         pass  1.48
Leicester            pass 10. 6     Market Harboro'        pass  1.54
Wigston North Jcn.   pass 10.12     Wigston North Jn.      pass  2.11
Market Harboro'      pass 10.29     Leicester              pass  2.17
Desboro' North       pass 10.38     Syston North Jcn.      pass  2.25
Glendon South Jc.    pass 10.43     Loughboro'             pass  2.36
Kettering            pass 10.47     Hathern                pass  2.41
Kettering South ]SL  pass 10.49     Trent                  pass  2.50
Wellingboro'    | &  pass 11. 2     Long Eaton Sta. )G     pass  2.57
Irchester South |GL. pass 11. 8     Toton Sidings   )L     arr.  3. 2
Souldrop        |     pass 11.16
Oakley Sta.     |     pass 11.26
Bedford Jcn.    ]     arr. 11.35

Toton P. Class 5 (4-6-0) BR Engine.
Toton Enginemen and Guard throughout.
To be marshalled - Engine - Brake Test Unit - 52 empty 16 ton wagons;
                20-ton fitted brake van.
Train to be examined on arrival at Bedford.
Traffic Inspector to travel with train.
_____
The following to acknowledge immediately on receipt of this Notice by
telegram to "Divisional N.P.Derby" using the code "ARNO S.N.1732" :-

M.P.DEPOTS  -  Toton

D.O.S.      -  Nottingham Leicester St.Pancras.

Y.M.        -  Toton Leicester W'boro' St.Pancras.

S.M.        -  Long Eaton Trent Loughboro' Syston Leicester Wigston
               Magna Market Harboro' Desboro' Glendon & R. Kettering
               Wellingboro' Sharnbrook Bedford.
_____
DERBY.                       L.P.BALL.
3RD DECEMBER 1952.      DIVISIONAL OPERATING SUPERINTENDENT.
```

later that year when another fully-fitted, on that occasion hauling 52 x -16 ton empty
wagons ran from Toton to Bedford and return with a BR Standard Class '5' locomotive.
He also participated in the Westinghouse braking tests between Trowell Junction and
Ilkeston South Junction. In 1995 for Bill's 90th birthday, I wrote to the Driver Manager
for Midland Main Line at Derby and secured him a HST cab ride to St. Pancras. It would
rekindle memories when he last worked over that route some 25 years earlier. He was
unaware of what was in store until a Traction Inspector ushered him into the cab of the
HST. I declined the invitation to accompany them in the cab and retired into the train.
Bill was in his element, his behaviour was impeccable and on arrival at St. Pancras the
Traction Inspector presented him with a book written by an engineman from Hasland
motive power depot, which, in addition to Toton also had an allocation of Beyer-
Garratts; it was a nice gesture. For a change of scenery we returned via Kings Cross,
Peterborough and Grantham (he worked via this route to Whitemoor) to Long Eaton,
the only disappointment was that Bill was looking forward to fish and chips in London
and owing to time constraints had to settle for a baguette. On the theme of the Beyer-

THE FLYING COLLIER

Nearly 1,200 tons of coal from the Midlands coalfields are being carried to London at 40 m.p.h. —more than twice the normal speed—in a new coal express, a British Railways experiment already holding out great hopes of success

Master and mate on the leading loco of the coal express: driver Woods and fireman Fox

To Brent's assistant yardmaster D. M. Smith this train was unique in his 38 years' experience

THE TRAIN that ran up to the signals and stopped on a Sunday afternoon in Brent yard, on the inner fringe of London, was carrying coal for a London power station.

Coal trains are nothing new to the staff at Brent. The footways and the sleepers of the sidings are thickly black with coal dust, for this is one of the mouths of the coal-rapacious metropolis. From the Midlands thousands of tons of coal for London are taken by train into Brent and other yards like it. There's hardly a day throughout the year when trains of coal-laden trucks don't clank to a stop at the end of their plodding journey from Toton, some 125 miles to the north.

But to the assistant yardmaster at Brent, Mr. D. M. Smith, this train was something quite unique in all his 38 years' experience as a railwayman.

It was 1.11 p.m. by the clock in the signal box. By normal running a coal train arriving at that time would have left Toton before dawn—taking over eight hours for the run. The seventy 16-ton wagons and the two new B.R. standard 4-6-2 type locomotives which made up this particular train had left Toton just three hours and 38 minutes earlier.

Some 1,700 tons of train, 1,120 tons of coal, had covered 125 miles in 3½ hours—less than half the time of the fastest coal train hitherto run on any British railway line.

Leaning out of the cab of *Venus*, the leading loco, driver A. S. Woods—a Long Eaton man with 28 years of experience behind him—wiped his hands on the engineer's inevitable bundle of cotton-waste and austerely admitted that they had touched 60 miles an hour at points on the journey. Fireman Dennis Fox, from Middlesbrough, comparatively a newcomer on the job, with a mere five years to his driver's 28, grinned and admitted that it had been a pretty fast run.

From the dynamometer car behind *Mercury*, second of the two big express 4-6-2 locomotives, a gaggle of technicians descended. They stood and muttered in little groups, walked alongside the engines and looked at the wheels. *Venus* haughtily blew off steam with a whistling roar. *Mercury* echoed her.

Behind the engines stretched the 70 wagons,

still spic and span in their brick-red paint, coupled and piped together as no coal train in this country has ever been before, fitted with vacuum brakes from end to end, to handle the immense load at such speeds.

The coal express is an experiment. So far it does not run on a regular schedule. On the way-bills it is down as a 'special'. Performance data is being gathered by the technical staff who ride with this train from the new mechanised sidings at Toton through to Wellingborough, for a 15-minute refill of water and quick inspection, and then on to arrive in London in 3 hours 38 minutes, from start to finish—3 hours 23 minutes running time.

The object of the tests is to obtain information to enable a decision to be reached as to whether in future all coal and other freight wagons should be fitted with continuous brakes as a means of speeding up the movement of coal and freight traffic on British Railways.

Apart from some teething troubles the new coal express is a success.

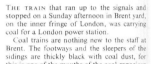

Two big new British Railways express passenger engines drawing a dynamometer car and 70 vacuum-coupled 16-ton wagons of coal halt in Brent yard after their high-speed run from the Midlands

COAL, March 1952   8

Garratts, described by some observers as being unpopular with fastidious drivers, indeed, a few did not take to them at all, even to the extent of requiring the locomotive to be turned so as not to run bunker first. Bill however revered them and recalled that before the introduction of these giant locomotives, the Toton-Brent services were double-headed by Class 3F and 4F 0-6-0 tender engines. It was the policy for the senior driver to be in charge of the train engine, this arrangement was to ensure that if the pilot engine were not available/required for any reason, then, the senior driver would still have the turn. Strange this, in some respects as the driver on the leading locomotive had charge of the brake. Bill and his brother Rowland, initially a guard and later a shift clerk in the Down Hump Room at Toton would often have a heated discussion over the loadings of the Brent coal trains. According to Rowland a 4F would take 47 wagons compared with 39 for the 3F, total 86 loaded wagons. Both were in agreement that the return from the capital conveyed 100 empties. The war years and after, saw Toton chronically on the block, particularly on the up side. Acceptance into the up reception roads was funereally

William Webb-Rowland Webb-George Bailey. Three old-timers with close to 150 years service between them.

Location and date unknown. A magnificent majestic Beyer-Garratt locomotive 2-6-6-2T No. 47991 with steam to spare. Photograph courtesy of Claude Cook.

slow, indeed, Bill recalls going out to relieve a train on the Erewash Valley, sitting on the engine until he was relieved without moving very far, only to find when signing on for his next turn of duty he would be relieving the same train, albeit some distance nearer Toton. A total of 33 Beyer-Garratts were built, the first three appearing in 1927 and the remainder delivered in the latter part of 1930. Allocated to Toton, Hasland and Wellingborough for the movement of coal and iron-ore traffic to the northeast, they also found their way to Washwood Heath and beyond.

The depots at Cricklewood and Westhouses also saw an allocation of these engines for a brief spell, but it was Toton that would always be associated with them. These huge locomotives could not be accommodated on any turntable and of the three roundhouses at Toton, Nos.2 and 3 were converted to house these engines inside the shed on the 'Garratt Road', whilst others were stabled alongside on dedicated outside roads. With the introduction of the Beyer-Garratts much of the double heading of the Toton-Brent coal trains was eliminated with the consequent loss of the London Pilot link at Toton. The London area had an insatiable appetite for coal; Stanton Gate Up sidings just over a mile north of Toton was where most of the Brent bound trains were made-up and despatched often hourly with a change of crew at Toton Centre.

As a postscript to the Beyer-Garratts, Bill would occasionally reflect on an incident when the driver and fireman were badly scalded after a steam pipe burst over the fire. After discussing this with George Bailey – I was his box lad in 1957 – he must have given

the matter some thought and wrote me. "While working at Toton East Junction signalbox during the winter of 1940, Garratt engine No. 7967 was taking a coal train from Sandiacre (it had been worked to that point from Stanton Gate) to Brent on a Sunday night. As the train passed the box, both the driver W. Hurley and the fireman 'Punch' Wooley, – who had taken over from the booked fireman who was sick – could be seen firing the locomotive. When the train got to Ratcliffe Junction, just over three miles into its journey a boiler pipe burst over the fire. Both men were severely scalded. The driver stopped the train and assisted the fireman to walk back to the guard. (There was a suggestion that the guard actually carried one or both enginemen quite a distance). The footplate crew were eventually taken to Loughborough hospital, but died later. To make matters worse there was a severe frost at the time".

* * *

Two photographs taken and developed by Bill many years ago, with one featured in the 1954 British Railways London Midland Magazine pleased him no end.

It was of a single arch brick bridge, built in 1872 spanning all four tracks, the only such type on the Midland Main Line at Sutton Bonnington (between Hathern and Kegworth). The other photograph was of the weir at Trent Lock that broke in 1953 undermining the abutments of the viaduct (see page 20).

* * *

As mentioned earlier 1966 was an interesting year, notwithstanding those immortal words uttered by Kenneth Wolstenholme – "They think it's all over, it is now!" – An unprecedented movement of condemned steam locos took place on 23rd January when a 'train' from Crewe to Kettering for G. Cohen & Son Private Sidings conveyed no fewer than ten dead locomotives. What a sight that must have been. Locally the Beeching Axe began to bite with the closures on 14th February of Borrowash and Draycott & Breaston stations where wee George Mellors had the honour of despatching the last train. Trent station would remain until 31st January 1967 (see overleaf).

At the beginning of April, I had an interview at Furlong House in Nottingham for the post of Assistant Controller (Passenger) Class 3 located at Leicester. J.A.McEvoy[1] presided over the interview and I was asked various questions appertaining to train running etc. We talked at length of the functions of the Control Office and I asked him if he knew Jack Galletley in the Line Managers Office at Derby, to which he replied that he did. Echoing the sentiments of Jack, whereby he told me of his willingness to have me

---

[1] Divisional Operating Superintendent

E.R.U. 18422

BRITISH RAILWAYS

THE RAILWAY EXECUTIVE
LONDON MIDLAND REGION

RGE DOW
ns & Publicity Officer   Your Reference   PUBLIC RELATIONS & PUBLICITY OFFICER

/. TONGE
Relations and Publicity   EUSTON HOUSE
Officer   LONDON N.W.I

—

lephone   Our Reference
1234 Ext. 254   AM 1   24th August 1953

W. Webb Esq.
53 Briar Gate
Long Eaton
NOTTS.

Dear Mr. WEBB,

        Thank you for your letter enclosing the photograph of the single span brick bridge which I hope to publish in a future issue of the staff magazine. Payment will be made when it appears.

        I am most obliged for your interest.

                Yours faithfully,

                for GEORGE DOW

Another location taken by William Webb that appeared in the British Railways London Midland Region Magazine in 1954. This is the only brick single arch bridge on the Midland Main Line that spanned all four tracks. Built in 1872 and situated at Sutton Bonington between Kegworth (south of Trent) and Hathern and photographed between the down and up main lines looking north.

PORTER Mr. George Mellers gives the green light for the " Enthusiasts' Special " to leave the platform at Draycott Station, which closed on Saturday night.

working alongside him might possibly have worked in my favour as I received a letter dated 22nd April informing me that I had been selected to fill the position at Leicester, date of transfer to be advised, it was signed by A.P. Watkinson, Station Manager, Long Eaton. This must have been one of the earlier appointments for Paul as he went on to become Director, Employee Relations at the British Railways Board.

John McEvoy was a gentleman, short in stature and habitually looked over the top of his spectacles when in conversation. He always gave me the impression of being a sincere person, extremely positive and well respected by most.

Another letter dated 3rd May from Furlong House reached me after initially being sent to Leicester, advising me that I would become displaced under the Nottingham Divisional Control Organisation – Amalgamation of Nottingham, Derby and Leicester Control Rooms. Attached to the letter was a list of positions that I could apply for in the Nottingham Control Organisation under the closed list procedure. How unusual, displaced, even before being transferring to the new post. At the interview I didn't recall Mac informing me that the Leicester office would be relocating to Nottingham, although I'm pretty sure that he would have done. A further letter of 13th May informed me that I had been appointed Assistant Controller (General Assistant) Class 3 under the closed list procedure. My transfer date to Leicester was 16th May 1966. So, after just over six years at Trent – the station would close on 31st December 1967 – it was off to pastures new.

Trent, to have been at the station without seeing or hearing a train was unusual, normally there would be some movement in the vicinity. Whether it was a train of empty iron-ore tipplers rattling along the high-level goods line bound for the Northamptonshire ore fields, or a freight train having come from a stand at Trent North giving its all on the way through the platform, determined to shout its way on the rise to Sheet Stores. The quite liberal view taken of the permanent 15 m.p.h. restriction through the station by British Railways fastest freight train, the 'Condor', with its 27 Platefit wagons making staccato overtures on the jointed track. The Luton-Bathgate motor car carrying service also hurried through the station and one night in December 1964, this train hauled by a 'Peak' diesel had eight cars blown off the carflats near Dent during storm force winds. The down 'Thames-Clyde Express' would also show scant regard to the 15 m.p.h. restriction, until September 1962 when a station stop was introduced. The unrelenting choking pea-souper fogs that lasted for days on end effacing all sounds, and the bitterly cold north/north-easterly winds, chilling the marrow to the bone. Trent could be a most inhospitable place, but I'm proud that I had the opportunity of being a part of it.

British Railways London Midland Region

Station Manager.,
Long Eaton.

Mr R.H.Fowkes,
Clerk,
Trent.

April 22nd, 1966

y/r
o/r Staff Pad.

Dear Mr Fowkes,

              I am pleased to inform you
that you have been selected to fill the position of
assistant Controller (Passenger Trains) Class 3
Nottingham D.M.O. (located Leicester) with an
allocation date of 16.3.66.

              Your date of transfer will
be advised to you later.

              Yours sincerely,

British Railways

y/r
date

to Clerk R.H.Fowkes
    Telegraph Office,
    Trent

o/r Staff Pad
date 10/5/66

from Station Manager
    Long Eaton

ext

Vacancy for Assistant Controller - Leicester

Please note that you are to take up the above post w.e.f. Monday next
5th May 1966. You should report to Mr Dann, District Controller at 09.00hrs
that date.

For A. P. WATKINSON

130/10/Rd/DyW **British Railways** London Midland Region

Furlong House
Middle Furlong Road
Nottingham
Nottingham 48531   Ext: 2279   R. D. Gardiner Divisional Manager

Mr. R. H. Fowkes,
Assistant Controller,
LEICESTER.

y/r
o/r   Date 3rd. May, 1966.

Dear Mr. Fowkes,

        Nottingham Divisional Managers Control Organisation
        Amalgamation of Nottingham, Derby and Leicester Control
                      Rooms.

    With reference to consultation meeting in connection with the
above.

    I regret when the above proposals are implemented, actual date
yet to be confirmed, you will become displaced. You will, however,
be considered for the positions in your own class in the new Nottingham
Control Organisation as listed on the attached under the closed list
procedure.

    Will you please return this list to me by Thursday, 12th. May,
1966 indicating thereon for which positions you wish to be considered
and your order of preference.

            Yours sincerely,

130/10/Rd/SW
British Railways London Midland Region

Furlong House
Middle Furlong Road
Nottingham
Nottingham 48531   Ext: 2279.   R. D. Gardiner Divisional Manager

Mr. F. H. Fowkes,
Booking and Telegraph Clerk,
LONG EATON, (located Trent)

y/r
o/r S3/-   13th May, 1966.

Dear Mr. Fowkes,

        Nottingham Divisional Manager's Control
        Organisation Amalgamation of Nottingham,
        Derby and Leicester Control Rooms.

    With reference to my letter of the 3rd May
and your reply.

    I am pleased to inform you that you have been
appointed to the undermentioned position in the
new Nottingham Control Organisation under the closed
List Procedure:-

    Assistant Controller (G.A.) Class 3.

Four

Out and About

1st July 1963. A journey to and from London was not without incident. With my night turn week in the Telegraph Office not starting until Monday, this was more or less a free day to get out and about. BR/Sulzer Type '4' diesels were then monopolising most of the Midland line services into the capital, steam however could still be found on the considerably slower trains to the metropolis over the Great Central line. Annesley (16D) had inherited a variety of 'Royal Scot' and 'Britannia' Class '7' locomotives, most in a poor mechanical condition. This particular day 'Royal Scot' No. 46101 'Royal Scots Grey' was in charge of six coaches on the 8.15 a.m. Nottingham Victoria to London Marylebone. A leisurely start, with the engine clearly not in the best condition culminated in a seven minute stop at Loughborough for a blow-up, before limping forward to Leicester where the recalcitrant was replaced by 'Stanier' Class '5' No. 44690. Leaving Leicester

Royal Scot' Class 7P 4-6-0 No. 46101 'Royal Scots Grey' no doubt having failed earlier, languishing in the siding outside Marylebone station devoid of steam. In front is Stanier Class 5 No. 45234 after working 8.15 a.m. from Nottingham Victoria on 12th August 1963.

Stanier Class 5 No. 44691 to work the 2.38 p.m. Marylebone-Nottingham Victoria on 12th August 1963. Train was 20 minutes late departing waiting the engine coming over from Cricklewood M.P.D.

On the Great Central line with BR Standard Class 9F 2-10-0 No. 92073 passing Lutter-worth working what is probably one of the redoubtable fast 'Windcutter' freights from Woodford to Annesley on 1st July 1963.

sixteen minutes late and with the loss of path between Aylesbury and Harrow-on-the-Hill, the arrival in London was twenty four minutes late. The return journey was also subjected to delay. I joined the 2.25 p.m. St. Pancras to Manchester Central as far as Derby. Hauled by BR/Sulzer Type '4' diesel No. D80 with eleven coaches, some five minutes out of London the diesel expired at Carlton Road Junction. There, a class '08' shunt locomotive came after a while to remove the offending diesel before another 'Peak' Class diesel No. D63 appeared to work the train forward, a thirty nine minute delay at that point increased to forty four minutes on arrival at Derby.

A couple of weeks earlier I had ventured to Brighton with its stony beach and pagoda style buildings for the one and only time. By push bike to Trent to catch the usual 6.57 a.m. departure from Trent (with breakfast included), now worked by a BR/Sulzer Type '4' diesel, then to the south coast before returning for the evening 7.30 p.m. from Kings Cross 'The Aberdonian' hauled by its customary Deltic as far as Edinburgh where an English Electric Type '4' took over for the final leg to Aberdeen. These two services were synonymous with the majority of my trips to the Granite City. With an arrival time of 6.38 a.m. there was just time for a coffee before boarding the 7.10 a.m. 'Bon Accord' to Glasgow Buchanan Street with Gresley 'A4' Pacific No. 60004 'William Whitelaw'. On that occasion I alighted at Perth to catch the 9 a.m. to Euston as far as Crewe. Sometimes this train was steam hauled as far as Carlisle, but not on that day. When leaving Aberdeen aboard the 7.10am 'Bon Accord' to Glasgow Buchanan Street, there were a number of options for services returning back home. They would include, Glasgow Queen Street to Edinburgh, where an excellent lunch could be had at the Station hotel, and then onto York and Derby. Services were also available from both Glasgow Central and St. Enoch stations via Carlisle to Crewe, or Leeds or Manchester to Derby.

The itinerary could be changed pending on time constraints and the type of motive power allocated to particular trains; the ticketing arrangements did not present a problem.

* * *

19th July 1963. A week's holiday to Torquay with Maureen and her parents, travelling on the overnight 9.48 p.m. Nottingham to Paignton hauled by 'Stanier' Class '5' No. 44981 with ten coaches. Leaving three minutes late with a further two dropped to Trent, there was a further delay at Leicester where the locomotive was short of steam. We departed twelve minutes late and came to a stand at Hinckley for some considerable time before 44981 finally succumbed at Water Orton. There we stood for sixty eight minutes before assistance arrived in the shape of 'Jubilee' No. 45585 'Hyderabad', which, running tender first hauled the train into Birmingham New Street.

Although no detailed recording, the train left New Street 126 minutes late, losing a further 13 minutes to Gloucester and was 145 minutes late from Bristol Temple Meads, after the mandatory locomotive change. Then, with a Hymek diesel in charge and dawn breaking 25 minutes of the deficit were recovered on the relatively easy timings to Newton Abbot. Nonetheless, the arrival time at Torquay of 7.5 a.m. was far more acceptable than the scheduled arrival time of 5 o'clock.

29th July 1963. A day trip to Llandudno produced 'Jubilee' No. 45618 'New Hebrides'; three days later the same engine had charge of a half-day excursion to Dudley Zoo, where I had not been since my schooldays of the 1950s.

(Left) The fireman having a break from the engine 'Jubilee' Class 6P 4-6-0 No. 45618 *'New Hebrides'* before departure from Llandudno with a return excursion to Nottingham on 29th July 1963.

(Right) As above. Maureen in sole charge on the footplate.

* * *

5th February 1964. A shorter trip to Aberdeen on this occasion, boarding the 'Thames-Clyde' express at Trent with BR/Sulzer Type '4' No. D157 at the head of a nine-coach train. Leaving four minutes late, matters proceeded quite normally until milepost 29, there, a dead stand of eight minutes under clear signals before regaining power. Just south of Harpenden station the 'Peak' expired altogether. There was a delay of thirty-five minutes before BR/Sulzer Type '2' No. D5208 appeared on the rear to haul the train back into Harpenden station. There, D5208 ran round the train and departed sixty-six minutes late and being brought to a stand at Dock Junction spoilt an otherwise spirited

Photographed from the Midday Scot on 6th February 1964. 'Jubilee' Class 6P 4-6-0 No. 45553 *'Canada'* draws its train into Carlisle Kingmoor marshalling yard. Opened in 1963 and replacing seven other yards in the Carlisle district, Kingmoor was only operational for around nine years.

performance by the 1.250hp diesel. Dashing down the steps and across the road to Kings Cross, to catch the 'Deltic' hauled 'Aberdonian' with eight minutes to spare. The next mornings 'Bon Accord' had Gresley 'A4' Pacific No. 60012 'Commonwealth of Australia' in

Waiting departure from Perth is Gresley 'A4' Pacific No. 60012 'Commonwealth of Australia' with the 7.10 a.m. 'Bon Accord'Aberdeen-Glasgow on 6th February 1964.

With watering completed and by the look of the exhaust a good fire, Gresley 'A4' No. 60012 'Commonwealth of Australia' waits for the right-away at Perth on 6th February 1964. Relief signalman Barry Richardson in the frame.

'Britannia' Pacific Class 7P 4-6-2 No. 70002 'Geoffrey Chaucer' on Polmadie shed on 6th February 1964.

Crewe North MPD. 'Britannia' Class 7P 4-6-2 No. 70046 'Anzac' with 'Coronation' Class 8P 4-6-2 No. 46245 'City of London' also out of steam on 16th February 1964.

'Coronation' Class 8P 4-6-2 No. 46228 'Duchess of Rutland' out of service at Crewe North MPD on 16th February 1964.

'Jubilee' Class 6P 4-6-0 No. 45556 'Nova Scotia' taking water at Crewe South MPD on 16th February 1964.

charge, the return journey being via Crewe after visiting the depots at Polmadie (66A), St. Rollox (65B) and Eastfield (65A).

16th February 1964. A day out at Crewe visiting the Locomotive Works, Crewe North (5A) and South (5B) Motive Power Depots, realising 'Britannia' Pacifics Nos. 70000/01/03/04/12/15/ 18/23/28/30/35/38/42/46/49/50/54 and 'Princess Coronation' Class Nos. 46228/29/35/48/54.

Having worked the 'Golden Arrow' for seven years before being transferred to the LMR in 1958, 'Britannia' Pacific No. 70004 'William Shakespeare' photographed at Crewe South MPD awaits acceptance into Crewe Works on 16th February 1964.

Stored with chimney 'sacked' 'Royal Scot' Class 7P 4-6-0 No. 46155 'The *Lancer*' awaits its fate at Crewe North MPD on 16th February 1964.

Camden (1B) was closed to steam in September 1963 and its allocation moved to Willesden (1A), where on 17th February 1964 'Coronation' Class 8P 4-6-2 Nos. 46239 '*City of Chester*' and 46256 '*Sir William Stanier F.R.S.*' were in company with withdrawn 'Royal Scot' No. 46114 '*Coldstream Guardsman*'.

'Coronation' Class 8P 4-6-2 Nos. 46239 '*City of Chester*' and 46256 '*Sir William Stanier F.R.S.*' would be having their final fling before withdrawal later in 1964.

Steaming well at Willesden on 17th February is 'Coronation' Class 8P 4-6-2 No. 46240 '*City of Coventry*'. This locomotive would also be withdrawn in late 1964.

17th February 1964. Willesden (1A) Locos of note being 'Britannia' Nos. 70010/14/20/29/31/34/43/48/52 and 'Princess Coronation' Nos. 46239/40/51/56. 20th April 1964. Prior to working the night turn on Monday, a day to Crewe and Manchester. 'Britannia' Pacifics on view Nos. 70017/24/25/30/33/46/49/51/52 and 'Princess Coronation' Nos. 46228/35/40/54/55/56. Returned on the 'Palatine' from Manchester Central to Derby behind 'Peak' D55.

6th May 1964. Another Anglo-Scottish trip with 'Peak' D112 on the 'Thames-Clyde Express', 'Deltic' D9010 on the 'Aberdonian' and Gresley 'A4' Pacific No. 60004 'William Whitelaw' on the 7.10 a.m. 'Bon Accord' from Aberdeen.

* * *

12th June 1964. Southern Region 'Merchant Navy' Class No. 35012 'United States Lines' came through Trent running light engine from Nine Elms en-route to Leeds to work a railtour, returning two days later, again running light back to London.

* * *

22nd June 1964. Another permit to visit Willesden (1A) depot, which at the time had an abundance of 'Britannias' allocated there, of which Nos. 70014/20/21/34/54 were on shed with 'Princess Coronation' Nos. 46235/39/41/45/48. Turned out to be a rather hurried trip as owing to a shortage of control reporters I was requested to cover Sheet Stores Junction from 7 a.m. until 10 a.m.

'Stanier' Class '5' 4-6-0 No. 45195 devoid of steam and receiving attention at Carlisle (Kingmoor) on 2nd July 1964.

'Coronation' Class 8P 4-6-2 No. 46257 *City of Salford* at Carlisle (Kingmoor) MPD on 2nd July 1964.

Almost the end of an era: 'Coronation' Class 8P 4-6-2 No. 46255 *City of Hereford* with No. 46257 *City of Salford* behind, awaiting their next duties at Carlisle (Kingmoor) on 2nd July 1964. Both will be withdrawn two months later.

Carlisle (Kingmoor) was the last outpost for the 'Britannia' Pacifics, No. 70009 *Alfred the Great* receiving attention on 2nd July 1964.

'Coronation' Class 4-6-2 No. 46238 *City of Carlisle* at its home depot (12B) Carlisle (Upperby) on 2nd July 1964. (1 of 4)

The shed staff at Carlisle (Upperby) certainly turned out their name-sake locomotive in good condition as this shot bears testimony, even though No. 46238 *City of Carlisle* had only a couple of months left before withdrawal. (2 of 4)

'Coronation' Class 8P 4-6-2 No. 46238 *City of Carlisle* awaiting further duties at Carlisle (Upperby) MPD on 2nd July 1964. (3 of 4)

With nameplates removed 'Patriot' Class 7P No. 45532 *Illustrious* awaiting disposal at Carlisle (Upperby) with 'Jubilee' Class 6P No. 45640 *Frobisher* on 2nd July 1964.

'City of Carlisle' at Carlisle (Upperby) (4 of 4)

'Patriot' Class 7P 4-6-0 No. 45512 *Bunsen* at Carlisle (Upperby) on 2nd July 1964. It would have another eight months before being withdrawn.

An unidentified BR Standard Class 9F 2-10-0 with a mixed freight approaching Nuneaton Abbey Street on 13th July 1964.

An odd pairing of Stanier locomotives as a Class 8F 2-8-0 pilots a Class 5MT 4-6-0 on a mineral train at Nuneaton Abbey Street on 13th July 1964. The leading engine had probably been coupled to the train so that only one "path" would be required. This was not an uncommon practice and was known as "saving a block".

*   *   *

1st July 1964. Yet another trip to Bournemouth and the Granite City, again using the early morning service from Trent with 'Peak' D95 and the usual complimentary breakfast. 'Merchant Navy' Pacific No. 35028 'Clan Line' was on the 10.30 a.m. departure from Waterloo with Pacific No. 34082 '615 Squadron' on 2.24 p.m. return. No deviation of course with the traction on the Aberdonian on this occasion 'Deltic' D9000. A drizzly morning saw Gresley 'A4' Pacific No. 60009 'Union of South Africa' at the head of the 7.10 a.m. 'Bon Accord' to Buchanan Street. Stopped off at Carlisle, visiting the depots at Kingmoor (12A), Upperby (12B), and then Crewe North (5A). 'Britannia' Pacifics in evidence, Nos. 70000/02/03/0/4/07/09/13/14/15/18/19/20/24/28/ 31/32/33/35/37/42/44/50/52/54, and 'Princess Coronation' Nos. 46225/26/28/ 35/37/38/40/41/45/50/51/54/55/57.

13th July 1964. A circular trip on the Monday at the start of the night turn week from Draycott & Breaston to Tamworth (High Level) then via the Low Level to Nuneaton (Trent Valley), then Abbey Street to Leicester and Trent to Draycott & Breaston.

30th July 1964. A half-day excursion from Nottingham to Dudley Zoo produced 'Jubilee' Class No. 45721 'Impregnable' with a ten-coach train, routed via Chaddesden curve to avoid reversal in Derby station.

24th August 1964. An extremely long day again prior to the night turn.

12.30 a.m. Derby-Bristol Temple Meads (7.5 p.m. ex Newcastle) 'Peak' D86.

6.25 a.m. Bristol-Exeter St. Davids (12.45 a.m. ex Manchester) 'Warship' D814.

12.30 p.m. Exeter Central-Waterloo 'Atlantic Coast Express' with 'Warship' D8XX to Salisbury and 'West Country' No. 34025 'Whimple' forward.

4.25 p.m. St. Pancras-Leicester (to Manchester Central) 'Peak' D98.

6.9 p.m. Leicester-Trent (5.7 p.m. Birmingham-Nottingham) 'Peak' D115.

* * *

2nd September 1964. As a result of the rationalisation programme drawn up by the infamous Doctor Beeching, I travelled to Leicester via the Great Central to ride the Leicester Midland and Burton-on-Trent line where the passenger service was being withdrawn on the Saturday. Also closed to passenger traffic on that day was the service between Nottingham Victoria and Derby Friargate when Ivatt Class '4' 2-6-0 No. 43091 with a three minute late start worked the 7.35 a.m. train from Nottingham.

* * *

9th September 1964. 'Peak' D112 on 'The Thames-Clyde Express' with 'Deltic' D9004 on the 'Aberdonian' to Edinburgh and E.E. Type '4' D263 to Aberdeen. Gresley 'A4' Pacific No. 60007 'Sir Nigel Gresley' had charge of the 'Bon Accord', continuing via Edinburgh Waverley, after lunch at the station hotel, by the 'Heart of Midlothian' with 'Deltic' D9018 and 'Peak' D131 from York to Derby.

* * *

Mention was made earlier of having breakfast on the 6.57 a.m. from Trent to St. Pancras. This all came about, when, late in 1962 a stop was introduced on the down 'Thames-Clyde Express' and alighting at Trent were the catering crew who had worked up the 6.40 a.m. express from Nottingham. A friendship developed and in recognition of providing shelter until their connecting train arrived, a can of freshly brewed coffee was forthcoming each morning just before 7 a.m. In addition, many a complimentary breakfast was enjoyed when going to the metropolis by that train, although as a gesture of the goodwill that was afforded to me, I did assist with washing of the breakfast pots.

* * *

29th September 1964. Fairburn 2-6-4T No. 42053 and four coaches provided the requisite traction and rolling stock on a further casualty in the East Midlands of the Beeching Axe, it was the discontinuance of passenger services between Nottingham Midland and Worksop the following month.

Further incursions into Scotland via the south-coast continued apace, but one trip in November 1964 was indeed the highlight of them all. Deviating on the outward leg, instead of going direct to St. Pancras I took a DMU from Draycott & Breaston to Crewe for a 9 a.m. visit to Crewe North (5A). Having cherished the Stanier Class '8P' 4-6-2 locomotives, since first observing them thundering through Tamworth some twelve years earlier with up to sixteen coaches in tow. Slightly less powerful than the 'Princess Royal' Class, all of the remaining 'Princess Coronation' Class had been withdrawn in September, and languishing on the depot was Nos. 46228/35/39/40/45/48/51/54, a sad sight of those once magnificent locomotives. Continuing then on the 10.11 a.m. Crewe-Euston (8 a.m. ex Blackpool) with BRC&W 'AL1' No. E3008 as far as Nuneaton from where E.E. Type ' 4' D323 took over. 'Deltic' D9019 had charge of the 'Aberdonian' as far as Edinburgh from where E.E. type '4' D359 continued to the Granite City.

What was about to unfold was beyond my wildest dream. Waiting at the head of the six coach 7.10 a.m. 'Bon Accord' departure from Aberdeen to Glasgow Buchanan Street was 'A4' Pacific No. 60007 'Sir Nigel Gresley' looking majestic as dawn was breaking.

The driver, Jimmy, a shortish fellow who I had previously passed the time of day with on an earlier visit to the Granite City invited me onto the footplate, an offer willingly accepted. This of course was the engine that the redoubtable Kings Cross driver Bill Hoole whipped up to 112 m.p.h. at Little Bytham hauling a Stephenson Locomotive Society Jubilee special on 23rd May 1959. No such heroics though on this occasion, leaving Aberdeen a minute late, 'Sir Nigel' had the utmost difficulty keeping his feet on this crisp November morning. Slipping badly and fighting for adhesion up the 1-in-96 gradient to Ferryhill Junction was both sight and sound to savour, watching a master at work was both an education and privilege to witness at first hand. Continuing the five miles of climbing along the coastline past Cove Bay to milepost 234 – a gruelling start indeed for a cold engine – Jimmy gave 60007 his head and the engine fairly romped away with such a trifling load. Despite a top speed of 80 m.p.h. arrival at Stonehaven was three minutes late. From there I reverted to travelling in the train, conscious of the fact that this had been an unofficial footplate ride, although on reflection extending it to Forfar station or even Perth would have been more advantageous. Incidentally, some months later I learned from the Shed Foreman at that Jimmy had lost the tip of a finger – trapped in the cab door of a diesel. In 1964 Aberdeen Ferryhill (61B) boasted no fewer than eleven Gresley 'A4' Pacifics. Whenever undertaking the journey out of Kings Cross on the 'Aberdonian', a no-smoking compartment was essential. More often than not with the blinds drawn it was self-occupancy although on occasions the Ticket Inspector did lift them after punching yet another hole in my ticket.

*   *   *

2nd February 1965. Despite the demise of the steam locomotives the interest in the Gresley 'A4' Pacifics was as strong as ever.

'Peak' D48 was at the head of the 'Thames-Clyde Express' which now was operating from Glasgow Central owing to the run-down and subsequent closure of St. Enoch. 'Deltic' D9019 worked the 'Aberdonian' with Gresley 'A4' No. 60009 'Union of South Africa' on the 7.10 a.m. 'Bon Accord' from Aberdeen. Across to Edinburgh for lunch at the Station hotel before catching the 'Heart of Midlothian' as far as York, powered by 'Deltic' D9013, with 'Peak' D141 on the 4.5 p.m. Newcastle-Bristol.

*   *   *

23rd February 1965. Early morning to St. Pancras, then across to Waterloo for the 10.30 a.m. departure as far as Southampton, on this occasion, hauled by 'West Country' Light Pacific No. 34082 '615 Squadron' instead of the usual 'Merchant Navy' locomotive. Returning to Nottingham Victoria on the 11.58 a.m. from Southampton (10.50 a.m.

Bournemouth-York) hauled by another 'West Country' loco No. 34079 '141 Squadron' as far as Oxford from where 'Hall' No. 5933 'Kingswy Hall' took over to Banbury. English Electric Type '3' No. 6797 worked the train forward to York.

*   *   *

15th March 1965. Resuming my travels North after a break of journey from Nottingham Victoria by way of the 8.25 p.m. DMU to Grantham that afforded a connection into the 'Aberdonian' worked by 'Deltic' D9004.

Gresley 'A4' No. 60009 'Union of South Africa' was in charge of the 'Bon Accord' from Aberdeen to Glasgow. In the vicinity of Stirling a Travelling Ticket Inspector examined my ticket and promptly confiscated it advising me that it had two cancel holes, a free excess ticket was issued and endorsed – ticket held for investigation!

*   *   *

31st March 1965. 'Peak' D128 to St. Pancras, 'Merchant Navy' No. 35029 'Ellerman Lines' from Waterloo to Southampton. As on the previous occasion returned on the 11.58 a.m. from Southampton to Nottingham Victoria via the Great Central line. BR Standard Class '5' No. 73029, through from Bournemouth to Oxford, there 'Hall' No. 6841 'Marlas Grange' took over before another locomotive change at Banbury from where E.E. type '3' D6796 worked to York.

*   *   *

2nd June 1965. 'Peak' D91 to St. Pancras, 'Merchant Navy' No. 35019 'French Line C.G.T.' on the 10.30 a.m. to Bournemouth returning to the metropolis early afternoon with 'West Country' No. 34077 '603 Squadron'. 'Deltic' D9017 worked the 'Aberdonian' from Kings Cross and Gresley 'A4' No. 60007 'Sir Nigel Gresley' worked the 'Bon Accord'. The 'Heart of Midlothian' had 'Deltic' D9012 as far as York where it was replaced by E.E. type '4' D280. Continued back to Derby on 4.5 p.m. Newcastle-Bristol hauled by 'Peak' D59.

*   *   *

24th June 1965. 12.30 a.m. Derby-Bristol Temple Meads (7.5 p.m. ex Newcastle) worked by 'Peak' D34 with D35 attached as far as Birmingham. DMU Bristol to Weymouth. 9.21 a.m. Weymouth-Bournemouth (to Waterloo) had 'West Country' No. 34087 '145 Squadron' whilst the 12.32 p.m. Bournemouth-Waterloo produced 'Merchant Navy' No. 35011 'General Steam Navigation'. Returned to Nottingham on the 4.15 p.m. St. Pancras-Sheffield behind 'Peak' D133.

During the summer a further steam hauled service had come to light, a Friday only 3.30 p.m. Crewe-Glasgow, run presumably to ease the pressure on the Mid-Day Scot. 'Britannia' hauled with six coaches and scheduled to cover the 141 miles from Crewe to Carlisle in 165 minutes.

*   *   *

2nd July 1965. 1.20 p.m. DMU Draycott & Breaston to Crewe. 'Britannia' Pacific Class 7P 4-6-2 No. 70010 'Owen Glendower' worked the 3.30 p.m. from Crewe and was replaced at Carlisle by another 'Britannia' No. 70008 'Black Prince'. Returned from Carlisle at 6.50 p.m. to Leeds (4.10 p.m. ex Glasgow) with 'Peak' D29 and 'Peak' D30 worked the 9.40 p.m. to Derby (8.55 p.m. Bradford-Bristol).

16th July 1965. 1.20 p.m. DMU Draycott & Breaston to Crewe. 'Britannia' Pacific No. 70003 'John Bunyan' had charge of the 3.30 p.m. Crewe to Glasgow with six coaches. Back to Derby on the 9.25 p.m. Glasgow-St. Pancras with 'Peak' D30 to Leeds and D157 forward.

* * *

23rd July 1965. 1.20 p.m. DMU Draycott & Breaston to Crewe. 'Britannia' Pacific No. 70054 'Dornoch Firth' put in a belated appearance for the 3.30 p.m. to Glasgow and left sixteen minutes late, nine minutes ahead of the 'Mid-Day Scot' with 'Brush' Type '4' D1838. Some spirited running ensued and eleven minutes of the arrears were recovered – 141 miles covered in 154 minutes – despite four signal and two permanent way checks. Back home on the 6.50 p.m. with 'Peak' D27 and D35 from Leeds.

* * *

3rd September 1965. 1.20 p.m. DMU Draycott & Breaston to Crewe. 'Britannia' Pacific No. 70012 'John of Gaunt' provided the motive power on the final day of the 3.30 p.m. Crewe-Glasgow. Leaving nine minutes late awaiting the stock from the carriage sidings, albeit with only five coaches, a special stop was made at Carnforth for water owing to the troughs at Hest Bank being low, put the train fifteen minutes late at that point. A right time arrival at Carlisle was realised despite five signal and three permanent way checks. The sixty-three miles from Carnforth to Carlisle were reeled off in sixty-four minutes start to stop. Overnight back to Derby on the 9.25 p.m. Glasgow-St. Pancras with 'Peak' D20 to Leeds and D50 forward.

* * *

9th October 1965. The day I got married and off to Bournemouth for a honeymoon. 'Peak' D116 from Trent on the 11.35 a.m. Bradford-St. Pancras and 'West Country' Pacific No. 34034 'Honiton' worked the 6.30 p.m. from Waterloo.

* * *

16th October 1965. Returning from the south-coast to Birmingham Snow Hill on the 'Pines Express' 10.6 a.m. Bournemouth-Manchester/Liverpool with 'Merchant Navy' Pacific No. 35011 'General Steam Navigation' as far as Oxford, Brush Type '4' D1711 replaced the steam locomotive. From New Street to Derby, with 'Peak' D34 working the 9.20 a.m. Plymouth-Bradford. There wouldn't be further trips across the border that year I had used up my allocation of free tickets.

However 1966 was to be an interesting year. The forays began again in earnest with some deviation and the 'Aberdonian' would no longer be used as a means of reaching the Granite City. 'The Bon Accord' 7.10 a.m. Aberdeen to Glasgow Buchanan Street had reverted to diesel haulage with NBL Type '2' diesel-electric operating as a single unit. Prior to the Gresley Pacifics taking over the Aberdeen-Glasgow 3-hr workings in 1962 the North British Locomotive Company's Type '2' diesels were being used in pairs, their availability was cause for concern no doubt exasperated by the company going into liquidation in the Spring of 1962.

* * *

16th February 1966. Leaving Derby at 7.50 a.m. to Carlisle via Leeds on the 6.35 a.m. Birmingham-Bradford with 'Peak' D51 providing the motive power. 'Peak' D15 was at the head of the 10.25 a.m. to Glasgow. The 1.32 p.m. Carlisle-Perth (9.25 a.m. ex Crewe) was steam hauled across the border; motive power being whatever Kingmoor (12A) saw fit to turn out, on this day 'Britannia' Pacific No. 70036 'Boadicea' had the duty. Alighted at Stirling in order to afford a connection into 'The Grampian' 1.30 p.m. Aberdeen-Glasgow that had Gresley 'A4' No. 60019 'Bittern' at its head.

After five hours in Glasgow, returned to Buchanan Street on a bitterly cold and frosty night to board the 11 p.m. to Aberdeen with 'A4' No. 60019 'Bittern' simmering quietly.

On exchanging pleasantries with the enginemen I was invited onto the footplate for a maiden nocturnal trip. With eleven coaches in tow there was much slipping on the 1-in-79 gradient through the tunnels to St. Rollox, the start being very slow in consequence. With a full moon, a crisp exhaust beat, what an exhilarating experience. A permanent way check and a dead stand at Larbert for signals culminating with a maximum speed of 75 m.p.h. before Stirling were the main highlights. The fact that the schedule was more generous than the 3hr daytime services was academic. From that point I retired into the train, cat-napping to Aberdeen arriving seven-minutes early at 3.13 a.m. on a relatively easy schedule. 'The Bon Accord' had now reverted to diesel haulage so it was now back on the 6.20 a.m. to Perth in the company of 'A4' No. 60024 'Kingfisher'. On earlier occasions the 9 a.m. to Euston could be steam hauled, not on this day though, with the usual English Electric Type '4' diesel I alighted at Preston and continued via Manchester to Derby with 'Peak' D45 working the 4.25 p.m. to St. Pancras.

In February of the final year of steam haulage on the ex-Caledonian route the doyen of the A4s No. 60007 'Sir Nigel Gresley' was withdrawn – and subsequently preserved – which put the survivors down to five, Nos. 60004/9/19/24/34.

*   *   *

14th March 1966. Trent to St. Pancras with 'Peak' D37, then across to Waterloo for the 10.30 a.m. to Southampton with 'Merchant Navy' No. 35008 'Orient Line', returning at 11.55 on the 10.5 a.m. Poole-York as far as Nottingham Victoria. Stanier Class '5' No. 45134 was working through to Banbury, from where English Electric Type '3' D 6747 came on for the remainder of the journey. By this time an engine change at Oxford had ceased.

*   *   *

23rd March 1966. Another sortie via the Settle & Carlisle route to Carlisle, with 'Peak' D27 working the 10.25 a.m. ex Leeds. Another 'Britannia' Pacific No. 70002 'Geoffrey Chaucer' re-engined the 9.25 a.m. Crewe-Perth with its usual five coaches. The 4.45 p.m. Stirling-Glasgow (1.30 p.m. ex Aberdeen 'The Grampian') yet again had 'A4' No. 60019 'Bittern' on the front. Overnight from Glasgow on the 9.25 p.m. to St. Pancras as far as Carlisle with 'Peak' D27 changing there into the 10.5 p.m. Edinburgh-St. Pancras to Nottingham with 'Peak' D12 (D39 ex Leeds).

*   *   *

14th April 1966. Outward again to Carlisle with 'Peak' D21 working the 10.25 a.m. from Leeds. Having ridden behind 'Britannia' Pacifics on the two earlier occasions, this time it was a Stanier Class '5' No. 45135 that Kingmoor turned out to work the continuation of the 9.25 a.m. Crewe-Perth. Changed trains at Stirling into 'The Grampian' 1.30 p.m. Aberdeen-Glasgow hauled by a gleaming Gresley 'A4' No. 60034 'Lord Farringdon'. Returned overnight to Derby by the 9.25 p.m. Glasgow-St. Pancras.

25th April 1966. Joined 6.50 a.m. Derby-St. Pancras at Sawley Junction with 'Peaks' D88 & D36 – this service was used for proving runs with Type '4' diesels attached ex-works – changing at Leicester into 6.55 a.m. Nottingham-St. Pancras with 'Peak' D56. At Waterloo on the 10.30 a.m. departure was 'Merchant Navy' No. 35026 'Lamport & Holt Line', which I travelled as far as Southampton returning at 1.13 p.m. behind 'West Country' Pacific No. 34047 'Callington' bringing to an end my steam journeys on the Southern. Joined the 4.50 p.m. St. Pancras-Bradford with 'Peak' D56 as far as Leicester, then by DMU to Trent and Sawley Junction.

* * *

25th May 1966. A final trip to Aberdeen. Overnight from Derby on the 9.30 p.m. St. Pancras-Glasgow 'Peak' D97 to Leeds, D13 forward. Across to Buchanan Street for the 8.25 a.m. 'The Grampian' to the Granite City hauled by Gresley 'A4' No. 60024 'King-fisher', the first time I had travelled by this service. Visited Ferryhill M.P.D. and returned to Glasgow on (another first) the 5.15 p.m. 'Granite City' with 'A4' No. 60019 'Bittern'. Back to Derby on the 9.25 p.m. Glasgow-St. Pancras with 'Peak' D28 as far as Leeds and D124 forward.

* * *

17th September 1966. The remaining Gresley 'A4' Pacifics were withdrawn, Nos. 60009 'Union of South Africa' and 60019 'Bittern' joining 60007 'Sir Nigel Gresley' in preservation. The locomotives had four extremely successful years on the Glasgow-Aberdeen route. Indeed, there must have been many a doubting Thomas when it was announced that ageing steam locomotives were to replace the troublesome NBL Co. Type '2' diesels on the accelerated 3-hour express services. Featuring tightly timed schedules with little to spare on intermediate point to point timings, credit must go to the enginemen at Ferry-hill, St. Rollox and Perth who put up creditable performances with the ex-LNER 'A4' Pacifics, not forgetting of course the maintenance staff at either end of the 'Caley' main line.

My tally of runs behind the 'A4' Pacifics over this route was nineteen, with lateness on four occasions, only one of which was debited to the locomotive. Listed:- 60004 (3). 60007 (4). 60009 (3). 60011 (1). 60012 (1). 60019 (4). 60024 (2). 60034 (1).

Five

The Rudiments of Control

Having been declared redundant even before being installed at Leicester as Assistant Controller (Passenger), which of course suited me down to the ground; Leicester was some twenty miles from where I lived compared with just fewer than ten to Nottingham. At this juncture it might be prudent to include the methods appertaining to the workings inside the Control Office.

TRAIN AND TRAFFIC CONTROL INSTRUCTIONS
OBJECTS OF CONTROL

The fundamental principle of efficient train and traffic operating is that the scheduled timings of trains in the working time tables, notices, etc. be maintained, the booked workings for Guards, Enginemen and engines be adhered to, and that the instructions relating to the classification, marshalling and loading of freight trains be complied with.

The main objects of Control are to maintain the booked arrangements to the maximum possible extent, to guide the working back to normal when out-of-course, and to modify the arrangements when necessary to meet fluctuations in traffic.

The Control in conjunction with other Operating and Motive Power staff engaged in train and traffic working will have the following general aims: —

(a) To ensure the expeditious working of traffic including empty stock.
(b) To plan and organise the current working of Passenger and Freight trains so as to avoid delay.
(c) To obtain the maximum work from engine power and trainmen by:
     (i) Punctual working.
     {ii) Using the fewest locomotives possible.
     (iii) Securing the maximum authorised loading.
     (iv) Incurring the minimum amount of light mileage or unrequired assistance.
     (v) Releasing engines promptly after completion of work.
     (vi) Making the best use of unbalanced engines.
(d) To regulate the working of trainmen to ensure economical working and avoid excessive hours.

All staff associated with the working of trains and the movement of traffic must carry out instructions given from the Control and must co-operate at all times to the fullest extent, by information, consultation and suggestion to overcome difficulties.

Station Masters, Yard Masters, Supervisors and the Staff under them are not relieved of their responsibility and must use their initiative in carrying out laid down arrangements. Departures from scheduled arrangements and the provision of power and trainmen, for any propose other than booked, must be made through the Control.

PASSENGER TRAINS MUST START AND WORK PUNCTUALLY and must not be held for connecting services, unless written authority has been issued or permission has been obtained by telephone from the Control, to which an early advice of such a possibility arising must be given. If a train arrives late at a station every effort must be made to regain the lost time.

FREIGHT TRAINS MUST START AND WORK PUNCTUALLY and must not be held, either for vehicles to be completed or off connecting services, except by permission from the Control, to which an early advice of such a possibility arising must be given. If a train arrives late at a station or traffic yard every effort must be made to regain the lost time and the station or traffic yard staff must keep in touch with the Control so that instructions can be given to achieve this object.

TRAIN CONTROL

The detailed regulation of trains in running must be carried out by the Signalmen (or Regulators) from information received in regard to the actual running, the working at their signal boxes and their knowledge of the requirements of the line ahead, taking into consideration the margins available for each type of train.

Signalmen will when necessary receive instructions from the Control as to ultimate requirements, thus assisting them in carrying out the detailed regulation. In certain circumstances, however, the Control Staff will give definite instructions to the Signalmen on questions of regulation.

Signalmen or others responsible for regulation must consult the Control in all cases of difficulty.

* * *

During the 1960s, diverting services to other routes was a deliberate ploy on behalf of the British Railways Board in cognisance of the Beeching Report in running down many of the lines across the country, which included the whole Great Central route. Also, the fact that people were using other forms of transport including the motor car, passenger numbers were falling and closures were inevitable. The GC main line would be losing its through workings to London, the last passenger train leaving Nottingham Victoria for Marylebone on 3rd September 1966 at 17.15, hauled by Stanier Class '5' 4-6-0 No. 44984. The station at Nottingham Victoria would close a year later and the remaining DMU service to Rugby Central, starting from Arkwright Street would cease on 3rd May 1969 when the ex-GC line south of the city closed to passenger traffic.

Leicester Control was housed in Granby Street, a stone throw from the Midland station, a compact medium sized office where around ten controllers per shift were assembled. I well recall Les Ellis a section controller escorting me down to the Midland station on the night turn, where we visited East, West and North signal boxes and then the station inspectors. Meeting and having a rapport with staff in the front line was of benefit all round.

Having previously held the requisite eight miles free travel allowance, it was then necessary to obtain a residential ticket for the additional twelve miles travel to Leicester. There was also a dependence on the train service to coincide with shift working. Early turn on Monday necessitated cycling almost ten miles to Nottingham to catch the overnight Edinburgh Waverley-St. Pancras at 5.47 a.m. the remainder of the week with a seven o'clock start the 6.16 a.m. from Trent sufficed, returning via Nottingham Midland to Trent or Long Eaton station as appropriate. The night turn was the most time consuming, having to leave home at around seven fifteen and cycling to Trent to catch the local DMU half an hour later. This early arrival at Leicester afforded time at the local hostelry to brush up my dart playing, whereby Harry Gregory travelling from Nottingham had an alternative rendezvous.

Returning off the night turn by way of 7.40 a.m. to Trent, arriving home some thirteen and a half hours later. Some Saturday night turns I would be booked off, this was fortuitous as there was no train to get me back home on the Sunday morning. Of the couple of shifts that I did work help was at hand. My colleagues arranged a light engine move to either Derby or Toton on which I travelled to Trent and on the other occasion I caught a ballast train. My spell at Leicester was to be even shorter than was anticipated, even though the moving date had been deferred by four weeks until 30th October.

I had been waiting since May to go into hospital for a hernia operation and was summoned to the Derbyshire Royal Infirmary on 8th September and was discharged three days later. At the time there was seven Railway Convalescent Homes owned by the employees of British Railways, London Transport Railways, Docks, Waterways and British Transport Hotels Ltd. who contributed to the funds. A Board of Trustees and various committees, the members of which gave their services voluntarily, administered them. Being a member, the minimum contribution payable through the paybills was 3d per week; wives were also covered by their husband's subscriptions. Taking advantage of this, members were actively encouraged to make use of them, the Homes, of which five were available for men, Dawlish being the most popular was my first choice. Not surprisingly, there wasn't a vacancy and I was allocated a two-week stay at Par.

*   *   *

In between coming out of hospital and going convalescing to Par, Peter Griffin who worked in the LMO at Derby – he, along with other controllers would transfer to Nottingham the following year when the HQ office relocated to Crewe – and myself made an overnight trip to Carlisle returning via the Furness line to Barrow. We reflected on this journey thirty years later, neither of us could recall the reason for the jaunt but an exhilarating footplate ride was long remembered. At Barrow in Furness we introduced ourselves to the driver of the 8.46 a.m. to Preston and having made our interest in steam known and that we were railway controllers, were offered a footplate ride to Lancaster. 'Britannia' Pacific No. 70011 'Hotspur' was at the head of a four or five coach train. Fog, patchy, but dense in places was still lingering as the locomotive romped away with its trifling load. The fireman offered Peter his shovel and with it fed a hungry 'Hotspur', I had to decline the invitation owing to my recent operation. Instead, the fireman sat me in his seat with instructions to sound the whistle each time the driver nodded on account of the number of level crossings and the prevailing foggy conditions. It may have been a long time since 'Hotspur' had chimed so incessantly over such a distance. It was music to the ears.

*   *   *

On resuming work in the final week at Leicester it was cheerio to some and goodbye to others, many controllers opted for working at Nottingham, a number would move home others preferring to travel, whilst a couple would be accommodated locally to more menial posts. To coincide with the closure of the Control Office a Train Controller (Regulator) was introduced in Leicester North signal box. A similar post had been created a few years earlier in Trent Station North signal box. And so to Nottingham, Furlong House, situated adjacent to the old steam shed in the heart of the Meadows, not the most salubrious part of Nottingham.

Harry Gregory who had travelled daily from Nottingham for a number of years benefited more than most from the closure of the Leicester office, living in the Meadows he then only had to fall out of bed to get to work. The five years spent in the Control Office together with the short period at Leicester were without doubt some of the best days of my railway career.

Six

The Five Routes into and out of Trent Station

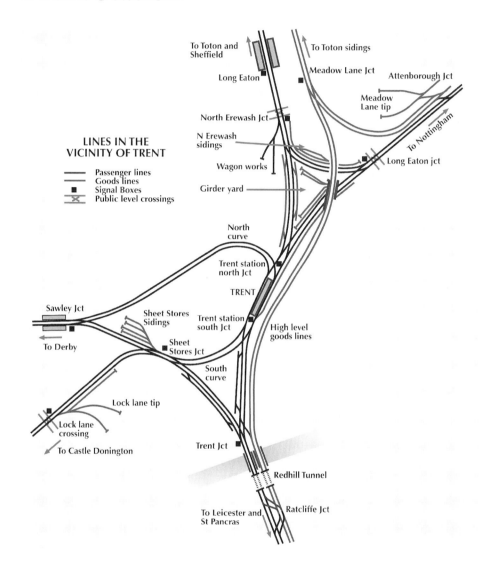

LINES IN THE
VICINITY OF TRENT

— Passenger lines
— Goods lines
■ Signal Boxes
⊠ Public level crossings

To Toton and Sheffield

To Toton sidings

Long Eaton

Meadow Lane Jct

Attenborough Jct

Meadow Lane tip

North Erewash Jct

N Erewash sidings

To Nottingham

Wagon works

Long Eaton jct

Girder yard

North curve

Trent station north Jct

TRENT

Sawley Jct

Sheet Stores Sidings

Trent station south Jct

High level goods lines

To Derby

Sheet Stores Jct

South curve

Lock lane tip

Lock lane crossing

To Castle Donington

Trent Jct

Redhill Tunnel

Ratcliffe Jct

To Leicester and St Pancras

(Left) BR Standard Class 5 4-6-0 No. 73067 leaving Trent with a semi-fast from Nottingham to St. Pancras. There were doubts in some quarters as to whether they would match up to their Stanier counterparts and in practice proved that they could.

(Right) 'Jubilee' Class 4-6-0 No. 45602 'British Honduras' takes a breather over Trent Junction with a Manchester-St. Pancras express in June 1957.

Route 1 Southbound – to Leicester and London

Fowler Class 4MT 2-6-4T will soon be entering Red Hill tunnel with a Nottingham-Leicester stopping train in June 1957. *J.A. Wade*

Up mineral train unusually on the fast line in Sutton Bonington cutting in April 1958 hauled by Class 3F 0-6-0 No. 43751. *J.A. Wade*

The signals indicate that the Beeston-Leicester freight with Stanier Class 8F 2-8-0 No. 48350 is having a main line run on 14th July 1958, instead of being turned onto the goods line at Ratcliffe Junction. Might that be a member of the p-way staff on the goods line viaduct? *Tony Smith*

Emerging from Red Hill tunnel approaching Ratcliffe Junction on the main line is Midland 0-6-0 Class 4F No. 44223 of Leicester shed (15C) working back home with a mineral train from Beeston on 3rd May 1959. *Tony Smith*

Local services between Nottingham and Leicester went over to DMU workings in April 1958. Cravens 3 car set passing Ratcliffe Junction with the 11.30 a.m. from Nottingham on 19th August 1958. *Tony Smith*

An unidentified BR Standard Class 9F 2-10-0 with a down freight for Toton approaching Red Hill tunnel on the goods line passing Ratcliffe Junction on 19th August 1958. *Tony Smith*

Route 2 Eastbound – to Nottingham/Lincoln & London via Melton Mowbray

Ivatt Class 4MT 2-6-0 No. 43016 approaches Long Eaton Junction with the 8.28 a.m. Derby-Nottingham parcels train on 2nd June 1959. The line off to the right and under the high-level goods line (Long Eaton curve) is to North Erewash Junction. *Tony Smith*

Ivatt Class 2MT 2-6-0 No. 46499 on an Officers Special which has just left Trent station on 2nd June 1959. In the background is the Girder Yard. *Tony Smith*

Fairburn Class 4MT 2-6-4T No. 42063 passing underneath high-level goods lines with the 4.54 p.m. Nottingham-Derby stopping train on 6th July 1959.To the left are Trent Girder Yard and the original main line that linked the north-curve. *Tony Smith*

An unidentified ex-G.C. "Director" Class D11 4-4-0 working the 12.10 p.m. Derby-Nottingham stopping train passing Long Eaton Junction signalbox on 1st June 1956. *Tony Smith*

A 3car Cravens diesel multiple unit working the 9.30 a.m. Leicester-Nottingham local passenger train passing Long Eaton Junction on 7th August 1958. *Tony Smith*

Midland Class 2P 4-4-0 No. 40337 with a Derby-Nottingham stopping train having left Trent in August 1956. *J.A. Wade*

Local stopping passenger train between Attenborough and Trent in May 1954 hauled by Compound 4-4-0 No. 41062. *J.A. Wade*

"Jubilee" Class 4-6-0 No. 45618 *'New Hebrides'* passing Long Eaton Junction with a Manchester Central-St. Pancras express running via Nottingham and Melton Mowbray in January 1955. *J.A. Wade*

Ivatt Class 2 2-6-0 No. 46502 on a local stopping train approaching Long Eaton Junction from Nottingham in August 1956. *J.A. Wade*

Hughes "Crab" also referred to as Horwich "Mogul" Class 5MT 2-6-0 No. 42784 near Long Eaton Junction on an excursion train heading for the Erewash Valley in August 1956. These locomotives being ideal for excursion and holiday traffic when not used for freight work. *J.A. Wade*

Running bunker first, Fairburn Class 4P 2-6-4T No. 42133 near Trent with a local passenger train in September 1953. The locomotive still sporting the lettering 'British Railways' in full before the adoption of the 'Lion and Wheel' totem. *J.A. Wade*

Derby-Nottingham local train nearing Trent in August 1953, headed by Class 4F 0-6-0 No. 43959. *J.A. Wade*

Fairburn 2-6-4T No.42182 with a Nottingham-Derby local approaching Trent in July 1956. *J.A. Wade*

L.M.S. design by Ivatt, Class 4MT 2-6-0 No. 43040 with a local train near Trent in September 1953. *J.A. Wade*

With signal set for the goods line from Trent Station North Junction to Long Eaton Junction, non-rebuilt 'Patriot' Class 4-6-0 No. 45518 *'Bradshaw'* eases its train for Nottingham over the junction in 1961. *J.A. Wade*

Non-rebuilt 'Patriot' Class 4-6-0 No. 45518 *'Bradshaw'* recently ex-works awaits the road off the goods line at Long Eaton Junction with a freight, possibly from Edgehill for Nottingham in 1961. *J.A. Wade*

Class 2P 4-4-0 No. 40553 passing Long Eaton Junction's starting signal with a local train for Nottingham in August 1956. *J.A. Wade*

The afternoon Nottingham-St. Mary's Class 'C' fully fitted goods hauled by 4F 0-6-0 No. 44223 on its way towards Long Eaton Junction in September 1953. *J.A. Wade*

Hughes L.M.S. design built under Fowler's direction. Class 5MT 2-6-0 No. 42761 with a west bound freight from Beeston in September 1955. *J.A. Wade*

Midland Class 3F 0-6-0 No. 43531 at Meadow Lane Tip. This was a regular Monday morning trip from Chaddesden that also conveyed the sludge tenders. *J.A. Wade*

An unidentified 'Jubilee' 4-6-0 well into its stride a few miles out of Nottingham near Beeston, with an express for London St. Pancras in May 1950. *J.A. Wade*

A Midland Class 2P 4-4-0 rushes through Beeston station with a Nottingham-Derby semi-fast express in May 1950. *J.A. Wade*

Compound Class 4P 4-4-0 No. 40935 with a Nottingham-Derby semi-fast express nearing Long Eaton Junction in August 1956. *J.A. Wade*

Class 4F 0-6-0 No. 44546 with a Sunday excursion off the Erewash Valley to the East Coast approaching Attenborough Junction in July 1956. *J.A. Wade*

Eastern Region Class 'D11' 4-4-0 No. 62660 'Butler Henderson' with a Lincoln-Derby express nearing Long Eaton Junction in August 1956. *J.A. Wade*

Stanier Class 5MT approaching Long Eaton Junction in August 1953 with a Nottingham-St. Pancras semi-fast express. *J.A. Wade*

Midland Compound No. 41143 with a Nottingham-Derby local train between Attenborough and Long Eaton Junction in August 1953. *J.A. Wade*

A Derby-Nottingham local train nearing Sheet Stores Junction in October 1957. Ivatt L.M.S. Class 2MT 2-6-0 No. 46440 in charge. The footbridge over the Erewash Canal on the left leads to Sawley, Ernie Phillips would often stop here for a blow-up when walking to Sheet Stores Junction signalbox. *J.A. Wade*

Route 3 Westbound – to Derby, Manchester and the North

West bound express at Draycott in August 1953 hauled by Midland Compound 4-4-0 No. 41069. *J.A. Wade*

Derby-Nottingham local on the approach to Sawley Junction headed by Midland Compound No. 41144 in July 1955. *J.A. Wade*

BR Standard Class 4MT 2-6-0 No. 76035 approaching Draycott with an afternoon fully fitted Nottingham-Derby St. Mary's Class 'C' goods in June 1958. *J.A. Wade*

From the fields near Breaston, BR Standard Class 4MT 2-6-0 No. 76086 is seen with a westbound freight for Chaddesden in July 1958. *J.A. Wade*

Locomotives mainly 4-4-0s and 0-6-0s awaiting scrapping at Spondon In September 1959. Two further lines of condemned engines are just discernible between the two signals in the centre of the photograph. The line off to the far right behind the locomotives went via Chaddesden and was used by the Midland Pullman to avoid Derby station and by the Lincoln-Tamworth 'Mail' to avoid reversal at Derby. *J.A. Wade*

Despite the influx of six Britannia Pacific locos, supplementing the allocation of the Jubilees, Kentish Town must have been hard pressed for the rostered engine as Stanier Class '5' No. 44690 was appropriated to work 12.25 St. Pancras-Manchester approaching Sawley Crossing in 1960.

Route 4 Northbound – to Chesterfield, Sheffield and the North

Johnson Midland Class 2F 0-6-0 No. 58173. Originally built in 1875 by Neilson and reboilered with small Belpaire boiler circa 1917. Photographed in April 1957 returning to the down main line from private sidings at North Erewash Junction. *J.A. Wade*

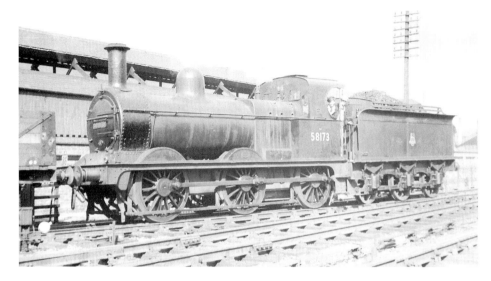

'Allo, 'Allo, 'Allo, what's going on here then? There's a calamity at Claye's wagon repair works in October 1959 as LMS '3F' 0-6-0 No. 43650 has derailed as it was leaving the yard. *J.A. Wade*

Johnson Class 3F 0-6-0T No. 47223 fitted with condensers for the London area, seen here shunting Long Eaton curve sidings, October 1956.
    J.A. Wade

Bradford Forster Square-St. Pancras express hauled by "Jubilee" No. 45639 *'Raleigh'* passing North Erewash Junction in April 1955. One of the few trains that did not call at Trent. This service was later routed from Trowell Junction into Nottingham and via Melton Mowbray. *J.A. Wade*

BR Standard Class 4MT 4-6-0 No. 75056 leaving Stanton Gate on the Erewash Valley with a Saturday football extra to Nottingham in 1961.
J.A. Wade

During the war years, and after, Toton was chronically on the block all along the Erewash Valley. Here, in later times ex-WD 2-8-0 No. 90152 is making good progress on the approach to Stanton Gate with an up mineral train in 1961.
J.A. Wade

Route 5 Westbound – to Birmingham/Crewe via Castle Donington

LMS Class 8F 2-8-0 No. 48333 on a west bound freight from Toton on the Castle Donington branch in September 1959. *J.A. Wade*

Following civil engineering works on the main line at Draycott involving the removal of two overbridges, all traffic was diverted over the Castle Donington branch. On Sunday 25th September 1959 'Royal Scot' Class 7P 4-6-0 No. 46103 'The *Royal Scots Fusilier*' has just passed Lock Lane Crossing with a St. Pancras-Manchester Central express. *J.A. Wade*

The Thames-Clyde Express

Up "Thames-Clyde Express" getting into its stride after leaving Trent station in May 1956 with Class 2P 4-4-0 No. 40542 piloting "Jubilee" No. 45615 '*Malay States*' which has steam to spare. The train locomotive is carrying the headboard. *J.A. Wade*

The up "Thames-Clyde Express" with Midland Compound No. 41100 piloting rebuilt 'Royal Scot' No. 46112 '*Sherwood Forester*' on the approach to Apperley Junction in September 1953. *J.A. Wade*

Holbeck was no doubt short of power on this day in June 1959, as Stanier Class 5 4-6-0 No. 44849 deputising for the rostered 'Jubilee' on the up "Thames-Clyde Express" coasting towards Trent. In view of this a pilot engine would probably be attached at Leicester in order to maintain time. *J.A. Wade*

Gresley A3 Pacific No. 60077 'The *White Knight*' heading the down "Thames-Clyde Express" near Apperley Junction in September 1960. Engines of this class were drafted to Holbeck (55A) for working Anglo-Scottish expresses north of Leeds during this period and had all but too short a reign. *J.A. Wade*

'Jubilee' Class 6P 4-6-0 No. 45664 '*Nelson*' coasts over the level crossing at North Erewash Junction with the up "Thames-Clyde Express" on 9th July 1956. Behind the wall on the left is Claye's Wagon Repairs. *Tony Smith*

"The Thames-Clyde Express" eases out of Trent station headed by 'Jubilee' Class 4-6-0 No. 45612 'Jamaica' on 1st June 1956. *Tony Smith*

The next departure on the clock from this platform is the 12.40 p.m. for stations to Nottingham and Lincoln. Rattling through Trent station taking a liberal view of the 15 m.p.h. permanent restriction is the down 'Thames-Clyde Express' in the early 1960s, on a very cold day judging by the heavy frost on the trees, hauled according to David Shaw the Telegraph Clerk by 'Royal Scot' Class 7P 4-6-0 No. 46154 'The Hussar'. *David Shaw*

Freight movements around Trent

Stanier Class 8F 2-8-0 No. 48271 now well into its stride passing over Trent Station North Junction with a Toton-Washwood Heath mineral train on 3rd May 1959.
Tony Smith

With clear signals through the station Stanier Class 8F 2-8-0 No. 48272 rattles over Trent Station North Junction with a Toton-Washwood Heath mineral train on 24th March1959. *Tony Smith*

Not long out of the 'shops', ex-WD Class 8F 2-8-0 No. 90362 passes the stationmasters house on the goods line from Long Eaton Junction with a Beeston-Washwood Heath freight train on 14th July 1959. *Tony Smith*

A Midland Class 3F 0-6-0 trundles towards Trent Station North Junction with a Toton-Washwood Heath mineral train, whilst another freight train also from Toton waits on the goods line. *circa 1959.* *Tony Smith*

This photograph, taken from Trent Station South 'box shows a Stanier Black 5 on the rise (1-in-586 & 1-in-220) to Sheet Stores Junction with the 4.28 p.m. Nottingham-Derby St. Mary's goods on 25th July 1956. *Tony Smith*

On its way home.
Northampton (2E) allocated
LMS Class 2-8-0 No. 48305
on the viaduct over the River
Trent with a southbound
freight from Toton in June
1957. *J.A. Wade*

An unidentified Stanier Class 5
4-6-0 on the up goods line
crossing the River Trent with a
train of empty carflats and
covered vans for
Wilhampstead in the summer
of 1960. *J.A. Wade*

Beyer-Garratt 2-6-6-2T No. 47974 gathers speed with a Toton-Brent coal train in April 1956 on the high-level goods line avoiding Trent station. Thirty-three of these engines were built from 1927 for the L.M.S.R. Since 1955 they had been superseded largely by the BR Standard 2-10-0s on the Midland Division. *J.A. Wade*

BR Standard Class
9F 2-10-0 No.
92122 leaving
Toton East Yard
in June 1958 with
a mineral train for
Wellingborough.
J.A. Wade

BR Standard Class 9F 2-10-0 No. 92024, one of ten that were fitted with Franco-Crosti boiler and side chimney approaching Meadow Lane signalbox, a short hop from Toton in October 1956.
J.A. Wade

BR Standard Class 9F 2-10-0 No. 92077 on the up high level goods line at Trent with a Toton-Wellingborough freight in April 1956. The 9Fs had begun to replace the Beyer-Garratts on the Toton-Brent mineral trains as the latter were withdrawn from service.
J.A. Wade

All ten of the Franco-Crosti boilered 2-10-0s were initially allocated to Wellingborough shed. In original form, exhausting steam through its side chimney, Franco-Crosti BR '9F' 2-10-0 No. 92024 is on the goods line near Trent with a Toton-Brent mineral train in June 1957. The locomotive is blowing off and the open cylinder cocks, together with the white exhaust, suggest that it might have 'picked up the water'. Trent station is away in the distance and the train is on the high level up goods line.
J.A. Wade

The signal appears to have been returned to danger rather hastily at Meadow Lane Junction as Franco-Crosti 9F No. 92024 gets into its stride with a Toton-Wellingborough freight in October 1956.
J.A. Wade

Beyer-Garratt 2-6-6-2T No. 47969 running bunker first with a Clay Cross to Wellingborough train of iron-ore wagons for the Northamptonshire fields passing Meadow Lane Junction in May 1957.
J.A. Wade

Midland Class 4F 0-6-0 No. 44131 leaving Red Hill New Tunnel in September 1960 with a southbound freight from Toton.
J.A. Wade

Midland Class 3F 0-6-0 No. 43624 still carrying L M S on the tender runs through Trent station with a mineral train from Toton, circa 1950.

On the High Level goods line is BR Standard Class 5 4-6-0 N0.73091 working a Leeds-Leicester Class 'C' fully-fitted fast freight.

BR Standard Class 9F 2-10-0 No. 92005 passing Trent on the High Level goods line with a rake of fully fitted vacuum braked iron-ore tipplers for the Northamptonshire ore fields.

'Britannia' Pacific 4-6-2 No. 70016 '*Ariel*' on the down High Level goods line at Trent with a train of empty 40 ton vacuum fitted hoppers from Stonebridge Park (Willesden) for Moorgreen colliery.

More used to hauling expresses on the West Coast Main Line, rebuilt 'Jubilee' Class 7P 4-6-0 No. 45735 '*Comet*' at Trent on 8th February 1964 with a delivery of coal to local signalboxes.

Ex-WD Austerity 2-8-0 with a train of Spanish ore from Birkenhead to Stanton Gate for the BSC works. The leading engine LMS Class 8F 2-8-0 No. 48672 had probably been coupled to the train so that only one 'path' would be required. This was not an uncommon practice and was known as 'saving a block'.

BR Standard 9F 2-10-0 No. 92016 with a southbound mineral train on the high level goods line at Trent in January 1956. *J.A. Wade*

Midland Class 3F 0-6-0 No.43631 passing Trent Station North signalbox with a freight for Toton in March 1956. *J.A. Wade*

An empty wagon train for Beeston is nearing Attenborough Junction in August 1953 with Class 4F 0-6-0 No. 44113. *J.A. Wade*

Passenger services around Trent

7.0 a.m. Cleethorpes-Birmingham leaving Trent hauled by Eastern Region Class B1 4-6-0 No. 61374 on 14th May 1959. *Tony Smith*

12.55 St. Pancras-Nottingham semi-fast leaving Trent station behind Stanier Class '5' 4-6-0 No. 45342 on 25th July 1956. *Tony Smith*

11.15 a.m. Derby-Nottingham local, approaching, but not calling at Trent. The signal routing the train over the 3rd down passenger line. Midland 4-4-0 Class 2P No. 40676 providing the motive power on 31st May 1956. *Tony Smith*

The lines off and onto the north-curve clearly visible as the 6.27 p.m. DMU Leicester-Nottingham leaves Trent station on 18th June 1959. *Tony Smith*

6.20 p.m. Derby-Nottingham formed 1X2, 1X2 & 1X3 DMU, leaving Trent station whilst signals are cleared for an arrival from Nottingham. 18th June 1959. *Tony Smith*

Coming off the 3rd down passenger line is Fairburn Class 4MT 2-6-4T No. 42146 with the 8.28 a.m. Derby-Nottingham parcels train on 17th June 1959. *Tony Smith*

On 9th July 1956 the 3.5 p.m.
Lincoln-Derby express leaves
Trent station hauled by ex-
G.C. "Director" Class D11 4-4-
0 No. 62666 *'Butler Henderson'*.
The D11s were then replaced
by ex-G.E. "Claud Hamilton"
D16 4-4-0s in 1957 before
they themselves were
succeeded a year later by light-
weight diesel multiple units.
Tony Smith

Midland Class 2P 4-4-0 No. 40411 leaving Trent station in March 1956 with a Derby-Nottingham express. *J.A. Wade*

In the vicinity of Sheet Stores Junction

With Trent Junction signalbox visible in the distance, BR Standard Class 9F 2-10-0 No. 92059 wheels the 3.5 p.m. Toton-Washwood Heath mineraltrain over the junction at Sheet Stores on 14th May 1957. *Tony Smith*

Local trains had been in the hands of Fowler and Stanier 2-6-4Ts and Midland Class 2 4-4-0s. The Midland shed at Lincoln had come underthe control of the Eastern Region and although a small number of LM engines were still serviced there, most of the through Lincoln-Derby workings were by ER locos. In July 1958 former G.C. 4-6-2T Class 'A5' No. 69824 is at Sheet Stores Junction. *J.A. Wade*

A freight from Chaddesden for Toton or Beeston sidings at Sheet Stores Junction hauled by LMS Class 8F 2-8-0 No. 48644. *J.A. Wade*

Seven
Photographs from the R.H. Fowkes Collection

Stanier Class '5' 4-6-0 No. 44672 passing Polmadie shed on its way into Glasgow Central with an early morning commuter train in 1960.

On a dank morning, a 'Royal Scot' locomotive Is running tender first to Polmadie shed whilst an unidentified 'Coronation' Class 8P (to work the 'Royal Scot') and 'Royal Scot' No. 46159 'The *Royal Air Force*' are running light to Glasgow Central in 1960.

Only a couple of miles out of Glasgow Central Class 7P No. 46159 'The *Royal Air Force*' is well into its stride with an express for the south. Photographed from Polmadie MPD in 1960.

The unidentified 'Coronation' Class 8P storms past Polmadie MPD in 1960 with the south-bound 'Royal Scot'.

'Britannia' Pacific No.70052 'Firth of Tay moving off Polmadie shed in 1960.

'Britannia' Pacific No. 70051 *'Firth of Forth'* receiving attention with 'Coronation' Class No. 46244 *'King George VI'* behind and a Metro-Vic diesel to the left on shed at Polmadie in the summer of 1960.

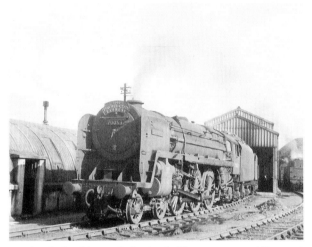

Two hundred and thirty miles lie ahead of the enginemen and 'Britannia' Pacific No. 70053 *'Moray Firth'*, as it prepares to leave Corkerhill shed in 1960 to work 'The Thames Clyde Express' from Glasgow St. Enoch.

'The Mid-Day Scot', running unusually without a headboard, 'Coronation' Class No.46246 *'City of Manchester'* takes water at Carlisle on its way southbound in the summer of 1960.

Carlisle (Kingmoor) MPD now recoded (12A) when transferred from the Scottish region, previously (68A), 'Jubilee' Class No. 45731 *Perseverance*. 1960.

Simmering on shed at Carlisle (Kingmoor) is Haymarket (64B) Gresley 'A4' No. 60004 *'William Whitelaw'* with Leeds (Holbeck) (55A) 'Royal Scot' No. 46145 'The *Duke of Wellington's Regt. (West Riding)'* behind. 1960.

A remarkably clean BR Standard Pacific Class 6P 4-6-2 No. 72007 '*Clan Mackintosh*' at Carlisle (Kingmoor) MPD. 1960

1960. 'Coronation' Class 8P 4-6-2 No. 46224 '*Princess Alexandra*' waiting to move off Kingmoor shed to Carlisle for a northbound working.

Two arrivals from the north at London Euston in 1960. 'Coronation' Class 8P 4-6-2 No. 46252 '*City of Leicester*' (left) and No. 46257 '*City of Salford*'.

Not all Western Region drivers liked the Britannia Pacifics, preferring their own Swindon built chargers. An exception to this were the Cardiff (Canton) enginemen who took to them admirably. Here, No. 70018 '*Flying Dutchman*' waits for the right away from Cardiff General in 1960.

An unidentified Stanier Class '5' 4-6-0 pulls out of Manchester Victoria with an eastbound express in 1960.

Coasting towards Manchester Exchange with a Newcastle-Liverpool express in 1960 is 'Jubilee' Class 6P 4-6-0 No. 45563 '*Western Australia*'.

Ex-WD Austerity 2-8-0 No. 90530 ambles towards Manchester Victoria on the falling gradient from Miles Platting with an up freight in 1960.

The Eastern Region G E line had an allocation of Britannia Pacifics from new, shared betweenStratford and Norwich motive power depots. Arriving at Ipswich in the summer of 1960 with a Norwich-Liverpool Street express is No. 70006 *Robert Burns*.

Having been watered, on arrival from Norwich, 'Britannia' Pacific No. 70006 will be turned prior to working back home from Liverpool Street in 1960 when Norwich depot had an allocation of twenty-two Britannias.

Reversing out of Liverpool Street station after working in from Norwich, 'Britannia' No.70002 *Geoffrey Chaucer* will be turned prior to working back to East Anglia.

Location and date unknown. Driver and fireman conversing on 'Jubilee' Class 6P 4-6-0 No. 45624 *St. Helena*.

The drabness reflects the general mood of 'not long to go' as Gresley 'A4' Pacifics await their fate at Doncaster MPD on 16th December 1963. Withdrawn in October, and, with nameplates still affixed are Nos. 60021 *'Wild Swan'* and 60025 *'Falcon'*.

End of the line for Gresley 'A4' Pacific No. 60029 *'Woodcock'*. Withdrawn in October 1963 and languishing at Doncaster shed on 16th December 1963.

Class 'A1' 4-6-2 No. 60121 *'Silurian'* on Doncaster shed on 16th December 1963.

Class 'A1' 4-6-2 No. 60139 *'Sea Eagle'* awaits the signal to leave Doncaster MPD on 16th December 1963.

Class 'A1' 4-6-2 No. 60143 *'Sir Walter Scott'* arriving on Doncaster shed 0n 16th December 1963.

'Britannia' Pacific No. 70035 'Rudyard Kipling' at Leeds (Holbeck) on 16th December 1963.

A Carlisle (Kingmoor) (12A) Stanier Class '5' 4-6-0 inside the engine shed at Leeds (Holbeck) on 16th December 1963.

One of Holbeck's long-serving 'Jubilees' No. 45597 *'Barbados'* seen here at its home depot on 16th December 1963. The locomotive was withdrawn in January 1965,

Photographed under the coaling plant at St. Rollox MPD after working the 'Bon Accord' from Aberdeen is Gresley 'A4' No. 60012 *'Commonwealth of Australia'*. 6th February 1964.

Stanier Class 5MT 4-6-0 No. 44658 running light engine, moves away from Trent station, circa 1950.

Two weeks later and 'Coronation' Class 8P 4-6-2 No. 46228 *Duchess of Rutland* and left, Jubilee No. 45721 *Impregnable* stored and 'sacked', neither having moved.

Class 4MT 2-6-4T passing Trent Station South Junction entering the station with a local passenger train for Nottingham, circa 1950.

Local stopping train from
Nottingham passing Long
Eaton Junction (later Meadow
Lane Crossing) next stop
Trent. The road on the right
leading to the station and the
rifle range, circa 1950.

Changing trains at Derby en-
route to Crewe. Mick
Chapman, Tony Slater and
myself, circa 1956.

'Jubilee' Class 6P 4-6-0 hauling
condemned loco through
Trent station, circa 1964.

'Britannia' Pacific 4-6-2 No. 70050 'Firth of Clyde' returning light engine to Leicester after working empty coaching stock from Willesden to Heeley carriage sidings passing Trent on the High Level goods line.

'Jubilee' Class 4-6-0 No. 45641 'Sandwich' for many years allocated at Nottingham now carrying a Burton (17B) shedplate trundles through Trent station light engine.

A return excursion to Leicester arriving at Rhyl on 27th July 1964 hauled by Stanier Class 5 4-6-0 No. 44666.

With Rhyl signalbox towering above the station canopy, 'Britannia' Pacific 4-6-2 No. 70051 'Firth of Forth' arrives with a returning excursion to convey day trippers back home from the North Wales coast on 27th July 1964.

Posing for the camera is the fireman off BR Standard Class 5 4-6-0 No. 73031 during a break on the Westinghouse brake trials in 1952. The photograph taken by the driver William Webb.

A view of BR Standard Class 5 4-6-0 No. 73031 on the 2nd down goods line between Trowell Junction and Ilkeston South Junction during the Westinghouse brake trials in 1952.

Driver William Webb at Toton on BR Standard Class 5 4-6-0 No. 73031 prior to working Westinghouse brake trials to Ilkeston in 1952.

Location and crew unknown. Shedplate is Toton (18A) Photograph supplied by Claude Cook.

Another photograph from Claude Cook's collection, again, person and location unknown.

Eight

Photographs from the Alan J. Wade Collection

Ex L.N.W. 0-6-2 Class 2P Tank locomotive No. 6917 at Edgehill M.P.D. in September 1947.

Webb 0-6-2 Coal Tank No. 27681 on shed pilot duties, Edgehill M.P.D. on 30th September 1947.

Non-rebuilt "Patriot" Class 4-6-0 No. 5543 *'Home Guard'* at Edgehill M.P.D. in September 1947.

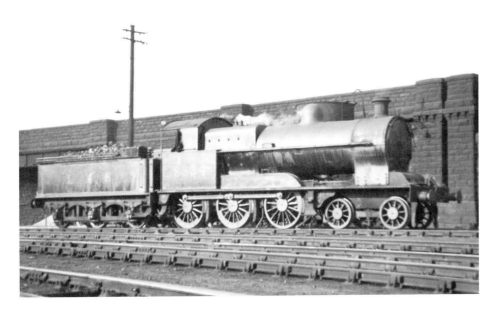

Ex L.N.W.R. Whale 4-6-0 Class 4F No. 8834 at Edgehill M.P.D. September 1947.

Class 6F and 7F 0-8-0 Nos. 8904 (front) and 9141 at Birkenhead (6C) M.P.D. in October 1947.

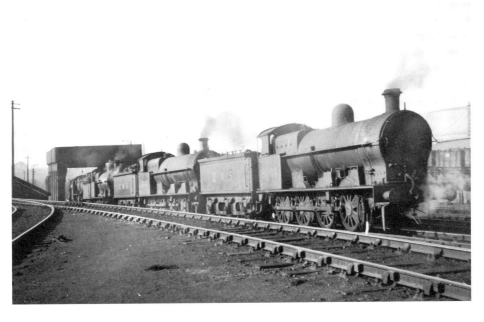

Aspinall L. & Y. Class 3F 0-6-0 No. 52164 shunting at Bridge Street Goods Depot, Bradford September 1953.

Aspinall L. & Y. Class 3F 0-6-0 No. 52236 at Mirfield September 1955.

Ex L.N.W. (Super D) Class 7F 0-8-0 No. 49048 approaching Mirfield with a through freight, including a rake of livestock wagons in September 1958.

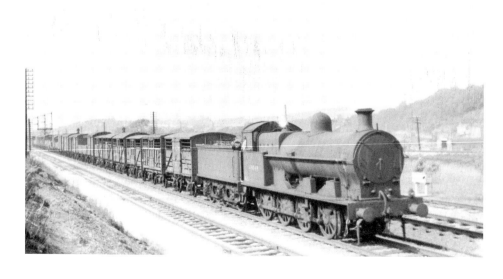

A pair of light engines, Stanier Class 5 4-6-0 No. 45329 and Fowler 2-6-4T No. 42377 on the down fast line at Apperley Junction in September 1960.

A delightfully clean "Jubilee" Class 4-6-0 No. 45655 'Keith' of Trafford Park (9E) passing Trent on a Manchester-St. Pancras express in 1952, one of the few trains not stopping at the station and ruuning via Nottingham and Melton Mowbray.

Class 3MT 2-6-2T No. 40139 in Newlay cutting with a Leeds-Ilkley train in July 1957.

Leeds-Carnforth passenger train with Stanier Class 5 No. 45265 in charge passes Apperley Junction in September 1960.

One of the once numerous Class 7F 0-8-0s on the Central Division No. 49674 trundles towards Mirfield in September 1955.

Fowler L.M.S. design, developed from L.N.W. G2. Class 7F No. 49668 running light engine near Mirfield in September 1955.

Ex-WD 2-8-0 No. 90295 ambles along towards Mirfield in September 1955.

An unidentified ex-WD 2-8-0 on an L.N.E.R. freight train at Gedling in June 1948.

Westbound freight near Mirfield in September 1958 with ex-WD 2-8-0 No. 90197. The bridge to the left carries the line to Robertown over the River Calder.

Former N.E. 0-6-0 L.N.E.R.
No. 2392 at Grosmont on the
North Yorks
Railway in May 1985.